"These wisdom-packed offerings teach beautifully how the new aspects of neuroscience can help illuminate what otherwise might seem like magic: The way we pay attention to the here and now of our experience can free our minds, enhance our relationships, and transform our brains toward well-being. Soak in these powerful lessons and enjoy!"

—Daniel J. Siegel, MD, author of *Mindsight: The New Science of Personal Transformation* and codirector, UCLA Mindful Awareness Research Center

"If you are looking for a handbook on how to improve the quality of your life, reduce your stress levels, and help build a better future for yourself, your family, your community, and your country, this book is it."

—Congressman Tim Ryan, author of *A Mindful Nation*

"*The Now Effect* reminds us how to have fun with our lives again. With his book, Elisha Goldstein has done his part to create the conditions for world peace!"

—Chade-Meng Tan, Jolly Good Fellow at Google and author of *Search Inside Yourself*

"*The Now Effect* shines with fresh simplicity and wisdom that will make you see your mind and relationships in a different way. A genuinely uplifting and very enjoyable book."

—Jeffrey M. Schwartz, MD, coauthor of *You Are Not Your Brain*

"In *The Now Effect* you'll get an invaluable map for coming home to the life that is here and now."

—Tara Brach, author of *Radical Acceptance*

"We all want to move beyond the dead end, conditioned responses that derail our best intentions and hold us hostage day after day, year after year; in these pages, Elisha Goldstein offers real tools toward that end. A wonderful book!"

—Sharon Salzberg, author of *Real Happiness: The Power of Meditation*

"Based on ancient mind-training techniques with a thoroughly modern twist, this book is a joy to read and even better to put into practice."

—Christopher K. Germer, PhD, author of *The Mindful Path to Self-Compassion*

"A valuable resource for clinicians, doctors, patients, teachers, and anyone else who is looking to rediscover and rest in the present moment."

—Pat Ogden, PhD, founder, Sensorimotor Psychotherapy Institute

"There's a freshness to the simplicity of Goldstein's approach that will resonate with those new to these concepts, as well as long-term practitioners."

—Tara Healey, MEd, program director, Mindfulness-Based Learning at Harvard Pilgrim Health Care

"In this elegant, thorough approach, Dr. Goldstein offers a clear path of inspiration and practices that brings the healing and empowering effect of the Now to every aspect of our daily lives."

—Kyra Bobinet, MD, MPH, Aetna Medical Director of Health and Wellness Innovation

WATCH INSTRUCTIONAL VIDEOS WHILE YOU READ

ATRIA AUTHORS ON YOUR SMARTPHONE

Tag images like the one above are placed throughout *The Now Effect* to bring instructional videos of Dr. Goldstein directly to your Smartphone.

To watch these videos, simply download the free app at http://gettag.mobi.

Then hold your phone's camera a few inches away from the tag images and you'll immediately be brought to the video.

View the tag above to watch Dr. Goldstein demonstrate how to use your breath as an anchor.

CLICK IT. READ IT.

Or you can watch the videos at:
www.youtube.com/NowEffect

the
NOW
effect

HOW A MINDFUL MOMENT
CAN CHANGE
THE REST OF YOUR LIFE

ELISHA GOLDSTEIN, PhD

ATRIA PAPERBACK

New York   London   Toronto   Sydney   New Delhi

ATRIA PAPERBACK

A Division of Simon & Schuster, Inc.
1230 Avenue of the Americas
New York, NY 10020

Copyright © 2012 by Elisha Goldstein, PhD

All rights reserved, including the right to reproduce this book or portions thereof in any form whatsoever. For information address Atria Books Subsidiary Rights Department, 1230 Avenue of the Americas, New York, NY 10020.

First Atria Paperback edition April 2013

ATRIA PAPERBACK and colophon are trademarks of Simon & Schuster, Inc.

For information about special discounts for bulk purchases, please contact Simon & Schuster Special Sales at 1-866-506-1949 or business@simonandschuster.com.

The Simon & Schuster Speakers Bureau can bring authors to your live event. For more information or to book an event, contact the Simon & Schuster Speakers Bureau at 1-866-248-3049 or visit our website at www.simonspeakers.com.

Designed by Suet Yee Chong

Manufactured in the United States of America

10 9 8 7 6 5 4 3 2 1

The Library of Congress has cataloged the hardcover edition as follows:

Goldstein, Elisha.
  The now effect: how this moment can change the rest of your life / Elisha Goldstein.
    p. cm.
  Includes bibliographical references.
  1. Meditation—Health aspects. 2. Mindfulness-based cognitive therapy. I. Title.
  RC489.M43G65 2012
  616.891425—dc23

                              2011033882

ISBN 978-1-4516-2386-4
ISBN 978-1-4516-2389-5 (pbk)
ISBN 978-1-4516-7229-9 (ebook)

To my wife, Stefanie, my greatest teacher, whose love and support continue to bring me back into the now, to what truly matters, over and over again

Contents

Introduction

A man lies dying in a hospital bed. He has spent his entire life building for the future, doing what needed to be done to amass wealth and raise his status to a level he thought worthy. Now he has reached the end of his days and finds himself filled with remorse rather than satisfaction. In his final moments, he turns to his doctor and says, "I spent my whole life stepping on people in order to get to where I want to be, and now there's no one left for me. It's only now that I realize it's so simple. It's who you love and how you love and the rest of it—the rest of it never mattered." That is a powerful lesson, yet he has little time left to make use of it.

He came to clarity at the end of his life; what if you could get this clarity now?

The psychiatrist and Holocaust survivor Viktor Frankl said, "In between stimulus and response there is a space, in that space lies our power to choose our response, in our response lies our growth and our freedom." What if an awareness of that space, that moment, could change the rest of your life? That's the promise that millions of people, including professionals in mental health, medicine, education, business, sports, and even politics, have begun to realize.

We have to wonder why Google, one of the most successful

companies in the world, offers a program to help its employees hone the ability to be more present. Why are health care companies instituting courses in engaging with the now for their employees and corporate clients? Why are a growing number of elementary schools teaching their children mindfulness practices? Why is Congressman Tim Ryan of Ohio passionately lobbying for the government to practice being here now? Why did Phil Jackson, arguably the most successful NBA coach of all time, encourage his players to practice mindful basketball? Why are mindfulness programs growing in more than 250 hospitals around the country and many more around the world?

The Now Effect is fast becoming one of the best-researched and most-talked-about phenomena today. Learning how to intentionally engage with the now isn't just a promised pathway to an abstract enlightenment but is becoming a practical way to alleviate stress and pain, cultivate emotional freedom, and even create a stronger, healthier brain.

Research shows that how we pay attention and what we pay attention to have a dramatic effect on how our brain grows. When we're on sensory overload, which happens often in our overconnected culture, we kick into autopilot to find relief. When we're on autopilot, our brain makes choices for us. So if we often entertain anxious thoughts, we're likely to strengthen connections in the brain that facilitate that type of thinking. If we intentionally focus on being present and more compassionate toward ourselves, we're likely to create a brain architecture that supports being kinder and more compassionate. This is real and powerful.

The way you wake up in the morning, do your work, eat your food, interact with your digital devices, and engage with friends, family, colleagues, acquaintances, and strangers over time all become routine. The ability to make things automatic enables us to function, but when life itself becomes routine, we miss out on the choices, possibilities, and wonders that are all around us.

Cultivating an awareness of the spaces in our lives that are happening right now is more than just moving along a pathway to self-realization, changing your brain architecture, or stopping your destructive behaviors. In this space there is a rich territory that has the potential to open your mind to possibilities you may have never thought existed before. You can become naturally flexible in your decision making, become able to regulate your body in moments of distress, calm your anxious mind when it's snowballing with thoughts, have greater focus at home and work, feel empathy and compassion toward yourself and others, communicate more effectively, and be more aware of what is most important to you. The secret is in the spaces.

the space between

In short, the Now Effect is the "Aha!" moments of clarity in life when we wake up to our truths. It's the moments when we come home after being berated by a customer and see our child running toward us, reminding us of our value. It's when we hear of a friend's family member passing away and reconnect to the loved ones in our lives. It's the moment we see a baby's smile and all our stress drifts away. It was on the sunny day of September 11, 2001, that many people around the world woke up and connected to what was most important. No matter how we get there, we find what is sacred and precious in life when we enter into the spaces of awareness that occur all around us.

Sometimes it seems like a cosmic joke that these spaces of clarity, which reveal the essence of life and our innate wisdom, are so slippery and so easy to become disconnected from.

The simple yet subtle truth is that life is decided in the spaces. However, the power to choose our responses comes only with an awareness of that space. As we practice becoming aware of the spaces in our lives, we soon come to understand that these are actually "choice points," moments in time when we are aware enough to choose a response. One response may be to bring mindfulness to whatever we're doing and break free from the ways of thinking and behaving that don't serve us. Mindfulness is the ability to pay attention, on purpose, while putting aside our programmed biases.

You'll be exposed to mindfulness practices throughout this book, but you'll also be turning the wheel a notch further, refining the focus with specific techniques that are tailored to prime your mind toward spaces or choice points. In a short time, those spaces of awareness will begin dropping in on you like moments of grace throughout the day, guiding you with more freedom to live as if it matters.

This is exactly what the writings and practices in this book intend to help you do.

When you think about it, there is no other time than now. Even our stories and beliefs from the past and our hopes and worries about the future are occurring right now. By doing the practices in this book, you'll begin to notice and engage the spaces in your life and not only experience greater clarity but, throughout the process, create new experiences and stories that positively influence the way you naturally see yourself and the world. You will be changing the way you think *before* you think, realizing the Now Effect.

It was a summer night in 2001 when I found myself doing exactly what I swore I would never do. There was a time in my life when I was living in San Francisco, working hard but playing *much* harder. I could often be found hanging out with friends at clubs south of Market Street, living what we called the "high life," experimenting to the point of abuse with drugs and alcohol. At the time, I was one of the top salespeople at a telecommunications company, and my mind always justified my behavior: "As long as you're doing well at work, everything is okay."

At some of the seedier clubs, there was a man I often saw who looked wasted away, as if the life had been sucked out of him, as he frantically danced all night—clearly with the support of some kind of speed. The mere sight of him would immediately make me feel disgusted. I remember turning to my friends and saying, "God help me if I ever turn out like him."

It was about 5 AM one Monday morning when I had been up for almost two days that I found myself in the backseat of a broken-down limousine with that very man and his equally strung-out girlfriend. She too looked like a shadow of a human being. If I'd had a mirror and my mind had been clear, I might have said the same about myself. I had intentionally sought him out at a club because I wanted to see if he had anything to help me stay awake long enough to get me through the workday. It was my darkest hour, and a voice began to percolate within me: "Please help me, how did I ever get here?" In that pain and desperation something became clear as the voice continued, "Your life is worth more than this; there are too many people who love you for you to throw it all away." In that moment I was thrust into a space of clarity where I knew what I had to do. As I jumped out of the car, I made the choice to walk all the way home and begin my recovery.

Though I'd love to tell you that in that moment I was transformed forever, that's not the way it played out, and frankly, when it comes to our deeply ingrained habits, it's usually not the way it plays out for most people. In the days that followed, my resolve began to weaken as I gradually stopped noticing the spaces of choice and began living on automatic again. It was just a few weeks later that I found myself engaging in the same old patterns.

The principles and practices in this book are what released me from being stuck in the habitual ways of living that didn't serve me, and gave me a life of greater freedom.

the top 10 benefits of the now effect

- You will literally change the way you think before you think and break free from subconscious beliefs and old programming that don't serve you.
- You'll have access to more choice points in life, bringing back a feeling of aliveness and opening the doors to greater potential, opportunities, and possibilities.
- You'll become more flexible in your decision making and responses to people and challenges.
- You'll increase your emotional intelligence and be able to relax more effectively in moments of distress.
- You'll be able to focus better at home and at work.
- You'll open up to feeling more grateful, forgiving, loving, hope-

ful, empathic, and compassionate—all key components of feeling good.
- You'll tap into the wisdom that lies within you and make your
  intuition more reliable.
- You'll feel more connected to yourself and others, a critical in-
  gredient of feeling well.
- You'll literally rewire a stronger and healthier brain.
- You'll change your life by breaking out of the habitual patterns
  of living that don't serve you.

I wrote this book to give you easy access to the essence of the
Now Effect and to show you how to apply it to your life. Part
I, "Getting Started," is meant to give you the best foundation to
prepare you for the rest of the book. Part II, "Training Ground,"
gives you the fundamentals to start experiencing the Now Effect. It
challenges you to bring these exercises into your life in a number of
different ways. Part III, "Know Your Mind, Change Your Brain,"
illuminates the reality of your thoughts, beliefs, and mind traps.
Doing the writings and practices in this section will teach you how
to break out of a limited mind and into greater freedom. Part IV,
"Priming Your Mind for Good," is where you begin to draw your
mind away from its automatic negative biases and nurture feelings of gratitude, forgiveness, joy, hope, kindness, compassion, and
resiliency. Part V, "Know Your Brain, Change Your Mind," gives
you insight into the inner workings of your brain. When you can
picture what's going on under the hood, it helps you move into a
space of awareness where you gain access to choice points to make
changes. Part VI, "Working with Difficult Emotions," is what all
the prior sections have been preparing you for. Learning and prac-

ticing how to relate differently to what's difficult are at the center of transformation. Part VII, "Getting Connected," introduces you to the reality of our interconnectedness, positively changing the way you relate to the people in your life. And Appendix A, "Deepen Your Practice," provides longer practices to give you the option to expand your experience. If you aren't able to make space for this section in your life right now, it's here for you when you're ready.

Most chapters in the book end with Now Moments, specific reflections and practices for bringing aspects of the Now Effect into your life. You'll also notice that certain chapters have bar code images in these sections. You can scan these codes with your Smartphone to be brought to a video of me leading you through a practice. To access these videos, simply download the free Microsoft Tag app at http://gettag.mobi. If you don't have a Smartphone, there will be links provided to the videos that you can type into your computer.

To give you the best chance for success for making the Now Effect come alive in your life it's important that you stay connected to a community of people who are also interested in this.

Take this moment right now to register for *The Now Effect* community at www.elishagoldstein.com and stay connected and informed as you move through the book with an option for daily Now Moment reminders, a weekly newsletter, and even a free once-a-month live call to help answer your most important questions.

I'm offering this to make sure you have the optimal foundation for making the changes you desire and giving yourself the best chance to live the life you want—right now!

This book is an opportunity to unlock the confines of your mind and begin a playful adventure. You will soon see the doorway into the space of awareness that might have seemed so elusive before. It's through these spaces that you will realize the Now Effect and begin to change the rest of your life.

Now take a breath, because it's time to get started.

part I

GETTING STARTED

ALL THE FLOWERS OF ALL THE TOMORROWS
ARE IN THE SEEDS OF TODAY.

—*Proverb*

You can think of the approach in "Getting Started" in the same way that someone might think of preparing a healthy garden. Under adverse conditions, dirt tends to become compacted. When this happens, it's difficult for water and nutrients to flow beneath the surface and for healthy roots to grow. The hardened soil also makes it difficult for roots to be resilient and makes them susceptible to disease.

All of us have had seeds planted in us from early childhood. This is our early programming; as in the garden, the soil often hardens around these seeds, getting in the way of healthy growth.

In order to create a healthy garden (and mind), we must prepare it for growth by breaking up the hardened surface and making space for the roots to breathe. After this is done, materials such as compost, wood chips, and grass clippings are added to keep the soil spacious, healthy, loose, and less likely to become compacted again.

In order for any program to create change in a person's life to succeed, that person must feel adequately prepared. I wrote this section to help you understand what truly matters to you and where you want this book to take you, and to introduce concepts that will be built on throughout this book, along with a simple practice to get you started.

The fact is, you are the master gardener of your life, and as you create a rich soil, you will begin to understand which weeds need pulling and which seeds need nurturing to cultivate a beautiful mind.

1

THE WISDOM IN GOLF BALLS

*It is not too uncommon for people to spend their whole
life waiting to start living.*

—ECKHART TOLLE

A professor stood before a philosophy class holding an empty jar. As the students took their seats, she began filling the jar with golf balls. When they reached the top, she asked the students if the jar was full. They agreed that it was. The professor then took a bag of pebbles and poured them into the jar, and they made their way into the spaces between the golf balls.

Again she asked the students if the jar was full, and they agreed that it was.

But the professor had another trick up her sleeve. She brought out a bag of sand and proceeded to pour the grains into the jar, filling up more of the remaining space. Again the question came: "It's full now, correct?" The answer was a resounding "Yes."

The professor then took a sip of her coffee and dumped the rest into the jar, filling up spaces that no one thought were there.

"So what does it mean?" the professor asked.

A witty student raised his own coffee mug and asked, "There's always room for coffee?"

The professor, along with the rest of the class, had a good laugh. Then she said, "Imagine that this jar represents the space in your life. The golf balls represent what's most important—family, children, health, friends, things that you're passionate about—the things that at the end of your life you would be glad you paid attention to.

"The pebbles are essential but less important, such as your house, your car, maybe your job.

"The sand is all of the small stuff in life that we're trying not to sweat.

"The coffee, well, you already answered that one."

The professor continued, "There is room for all of this only if you put the golf balls in first. If you put the sand or pebbles in first, there won't be room for the golf balls. The way we pay attention to our lives works the same way. If you spend your attention or mental space sweating the small stuff in life, you won't have the capacity to pay attention to what is most important to you."

This is a classic story that speaks to becoming more mindful of what really matters. I do the same exercise with my clients and students. Why? Thoughts of what is most valuable fly into and out of our minds all the time, and we don't see the space between our awareness and these thoughts. This exercise provides a physical representation of thinking about what really matters and simultaneously makes us aware of the space in which we have the opportunity to choose a response. The practice of intentionally paying attention to what matters primes the mind to become more aware of what is meaningful.

The biggest question at this stage of the process is, what in life really matters to you? Is it your relationship to your partner, paying attention to your children, taking care of your body, sharpening your mind, being kind to yourself or others, making room for play, or living with greater ease?

Paying attention to the things that you value in life is fundamental to your happiness. We know that our minds have an inclination to follow the path of least resistance, so we need a compass to help us intentionally come back to our priorities.

now moment

Creating a way to be aware of our values can help us break out of autopilot and guide us back to what really matters.

1. Sit in a space to take care of the golf balls first—the things that really matter. What are your priorities in life? Let's bring some awareness to them, because at the end of the day, the rest is just sand. Make a list in your mind or write down what truly matters.

2. Sitting exercise: Take a few moments to relax, close your eyes, and practice "Breathing in, I am aware of what truly matters, breathing out, I let go of living on automatic."

3. Go find a jar and a box of golf balls or some nice stones. Label each golf ball or stone with something that really matters in your life. If you don't have a physical jar, you can draw a picture of a jar on a piece of paper along with golf balls or stones or perhaps just picture them in your mind. Actions speak louder than words, so check to see where in your life you're bringing action to your values. Maybe you're taking

your partner out to dinner, responding to people and yourself with greater kindness and compassion, being less judgmental, playing games with your kids, getting back into exercise or yoga, making space for that round of eighteen holes, or spending time in meditation.

4. Put the jar in a prominent place somewhere in your house or office where you can't miss looking at it. Every time you intentionally look at the jar, your mind is more likely to incline toward what truly matters. As you do this, you prime your mind to respond to those values during the spaces of your daily life.

2

PAYING ATTENTION TO YOUR INTENTION

Life is the sum of all your choices.

—GOETHE

The two primary elements that shape our lives and can help guide us into the now are *attention* and *intention*. Numerous teachers from the world's wisdom traditions and my personal experience have taught me that intention is the root of all actions—that our intentions shape our thoughts, words, and actions. There's an old Tibetan proverb that says, "Everything rests at the tip of motivation."

Our intention is at the root of why we do anything and plays a fundamental role in helping us cultivate a life of happiness or unhappiness. If we set an intention for well-being and place it at the center of our life, we are more likely to be guided toward it. If we bring awareness to something, we connect to it. If we pay attention to our bodies or emotions, we are connecting with and attuning to ourselves in that moment. If we pay attention to another person, we are connecting with and attuning to that person.

For example, when I'm connected to my body I'm able to notice when my shoulders are getting tense or my body is feeling tired, and in that space of awareness I can take care of myself. However, when I'm disconnected, my mind is on autopilot and I'll just continue acting in unhealthy ways.

The fact is, when we're not aware of our intention, we're more likely to feel disconnected; get hooked into old, unhealthy patterns that don't serve us; and miss the space of awareness to consider a wiser perspective and response. When we make the choice to reconnect, not only are we more likely to make healthier and wiser choices, but we actually feel happier.

You can use this simple model that I adapted from psychologists Richard Schwartz and Shauna Shapiro to create a map in your mind of how this works:

Intention → Attention → Connection → Balance
→ Health → Happiness

Intention is our starting point, but in order to be aware of our intention we must focus our attention on it.

now moment

Right now is a "choice point," a space in time when you can choose to pay attention to your intention and get in touch with the sincerity of your heart and mind. Often when we try to really connect to our intentions, it's natural for judgments to arise, such as "This isn't going to help," "I'm too busy for this," or "I don't deserve real happiness." These are defenses to keep you from moving toward greater emotional freedom. If they arise, take note of them as best you can and set them aside. You can always come back to them later, as they might serve as helpful material. Then return to this practice, if only for a few moments, and become aware of your intention.

To become clearer on your intention, reflect on the following questions:

1. What do you hope to learn or change in your life? Do you want a sense of peace, more compassion toward yourself, a deeper sense of how to navigate the personal storms of life with greater ease and wisdom?

2. Keep coming back to this exercise throughout the day. Ask yourself, "What is my intention right now?" If you're not doing what you intend to do, without judgment, gently redirect your attention and actions.

3

UNDERSTANDING WHAT
REALLY MOTIVATES YOU

In my previous career in sales and management, my employers provided heavy financial incentives and trips to try to motivate their employees. Sounds pretty good, right? We thought so, but what the company didn't know was that focusing on external rewards (for example, money, trips, cars, and so on) was far less motivating than helping us cultivate an awareness of internal rewards (for example, autonomy, mastery, and purpose).

What motivational theory has found is that intrinsic factors are the best predictors of personal success for both adults and children. Many experts now suggest that we help children engage in activities that interest them rather than focusing on an allowance or prizes.

It's also important to understand that when it comes to motivation, the inner wisdom that arises from our own experience is far superior to an expert's advice. When I was a kid, my parents gave me their expert advice, warning me not to stick my finger in the socket that the lightbulb went into, but I wasn't motivated to stop until I actually got shocked.

The health care industry understands that external advice or rewards don't work well so they're starting to help people cultivate the awareness to find rewards within. "Healing is about a person taking charge of themselves and giving them the skills and abilities to do so," Kyra Bobinet, MD, MPH, Aetna's medical director for health and wellness innovation, told me. That is why she's initiating mindfulness programs in the health care industry to help people change the inner workings of their minds and perceptions so that they can access their internal motivation and effectively take action.

As you move through this book, I want you to consider not swallowing my advice whole but trusting your experience and allowing that to be your compass. I'll provide the map, but your experience in the territory is what truly matters.

now moment

Breathe in, breathe out; you're entering into a space called "here." In this space you can choose to do these three steps to define and refine what motivates you to realize the Now Effect.

1. FIND IT. What are you dissatisfied with? Take a moment to really consider what brought you to this book. Be specific; this is important if you have the desire to change.
2. LIST IT. Create a detailed list of what motivates you. Notice that "I just want more money" is unlikely to be as meaningful as choosing something intrinsic, such as "I want to be more ef-

fective in dealing with stress." Or maybe you want to experience more ease and peace or learn how to love yourself for the first time. Write out the list and come back to it often, as it will be a continuous source of motivation.

3. VISUALIZE IT. Albert Einstein said, "Imagination is everything. It is the preview of life's coming attractions." Take a few seconds to sit down and scan your body, letting any tension dissolve. Then visualize the areas of your life that are sources of stress or dissatisfaction. Now imagine what life would be like if you were able to notice the space before you react and meet your challenges with greater ease? See if you can feel the feelings that are present in this space. Take a moment with this.

4. COMMIT TO IT. Dr. Martin Luther King, Jr., said, "Take the first step in faith. You don't have to see the whole staircase. Just take the first step." Changing old habits can be difficult; that's no secret. However, to realize the Now Effect, it's important to make a commitment to engage in the practices consistently as you move through the book. The length or duration of practice is less important than doing it regularly. You can aspire to practice daily, but just take it one step at a time.

We all know that commitments can be broken, so what should you do if you break your commitment? Gently invite yourself back to the practice of being in the now. Self-blame is not going to move you closer to reengaging and experiencing the Now Effect. If it's not possible to return to the practice right away, invite yourself to make a plan to practice soon.

Know that each time you engage in the practices in this book, you are sending the message internally that you care about yourself; this is powerful nutrition for both your mind and your body.

4

PLAYFUL DISCIPLINE

Don't take life too seriously. You'll never get out alive.

—ELBERT HUBBARD

Being too serious distracts us from the experience of life; it sucks away our vitality and ability to be happy." That is what Chade-Meng Tan told me. During the early days of Google, Meng was one of the lead engineers responsible for search quality. One day while walking into a meeting, the Google executives were considering calling the highest-level engineers "fellows." Meng perked up and in a playful manner said, "Well, then, I'm the Jolly Good Fellow (which nobody can deny)." The name stuck, and he has since been known as the Jolly Good Fellow. Being around Meng, you can tell he really embodies this message, often bringing humor to any given situation.

Playfulness is part of the foundation of the writings and practices of *The Now Effect*. Somewhere along the way to adulthood, we lose our sense of play, and when it comes to improving our lives we can easily fall into a state of being overly strict with ourselves and taking it all too seriously. On the flip side, we can find ourselves being overly nonchalant and not devoted enough to the changes we are trying to make, which often leads to a lack of follow-through, experience, and depth.

As you engage in the writings and practices in this book, I suggest approaching them with a *playful discipline,* committing yourself to following through and bringing them alive by setting aside your lenses of judgment, being open to new experience, and welcoming what you find. From time to time you may stray from engaging with *The Now Effect.* As this happens, bring a bit of lightness and kindness into the picture, gently guiding yourself back to the practices. Doing this work as a playful discipline will create fertile ground for a healthy mind and make it easier for the Now Effect to take root.

SEE, TOUCH, GO

One day my client Laura came in to see me and was so happy she could barely contain herself. She had been asking her parents for a dog for more than a year, and on her thirteenth birthday Spot arrived. He was a rescue dog, a Springer Spaniel who seemed to want nothing more than to jump on her lap and lick every inch of her hand when she petted him. As the weeks went by, the family began to notice that Spot had never been trained before and would chew on some of the furniture, pee in the corners of the house, and bark when it was time to be quiet. The family was starting to lose their minds and began a process of training Spot so he would obey. But Spot had been practicing these habits for quite some time, and he had other plans.

The family decided to hire a trainer but after a few weeks didn't see any improvements. Little Laura became so frustrated, hating Spot at times, and feeling like she didn't want to play with him anymore. Her parents didn't know what to do either; they felt incompetent and helpless and wondered whether maybe they should give him back to the pound. They felt stuck.

One day during a family session I asked them to tell me more about how they interacted with the dog. Laura's mom said, "I get so frustrated, I feel like wringing his neck sometimes. I don't think things will ever change." In that moment I realized the difficulty was not only with Spot, but with how the family was relating to him. While I was not a dog trainer, I asked them to try a new approach when trying to train Spot. "It's important to know that training a dog is a playful process, and while he may sit at times, he'll also wander back to past behaviors like peeing, chewing, and barking. When he sees you getting frustrated or upset, that scares and stirs him up more, making it more difficult to adhere to his training. So part of this process is learning how to work with your own impatience, restlessness, and frustration.

"I recommend a simple phrase, 'See, touch, go,' that has done wonders to help me be more flexible in my life when it comes to changing deeply ingrained destructive habits. When your mind begins to wander off onto all your worries and frustrations with this dog, see that your mind has wandered, touch the thought like you might softly touch your reflection in a pond, and then gently go back to focusing on the work you're doing with the trainer." Over time, the family began to put a playful effort into working with Spot, and while he still had his mishaps from time to time, his behavior improved and he became a source of love in their house.

One of the leading figures in bringing mindfulness to America, Jack Kornfield, often compares the work of training the mind in mindfulness to the work of training a puppy. Your mind and behavior will naturally wander many, many times while reading and practicing the Now Effect. In fact, the psychologist Daniel Gilbert and his doctoral student at the time, Matthew Killingsworth, at Harvard University, did a study that used an iPhone app to randomly sample people's thoughts, feelings, and actions. After almost a quarter million responses, they found that our minds wander about 47 percent of the time (only 10 percent while we're having sex, if you can imagine how they tracked that), and there is a positive connection between focusing our attention and our level of happiness.

"See, touch, go" is a simple phrase to remind you to be present and is an effective way to relate to your mind and the practices.

now moment

It's time to introduce "The breath as an anchor," a simple practice that will get you started in training your mind to pay attention and give you the opportunity to work with "See, touch, go." Though it is helpful to carve out some space for quiet and concentration, "The breath as an anchor" can be done anywhere and anytime; that's the beauty of it. This practice can be done for thirty seconds, one minute, five minutes, or longer.

www.youtube.com/NowEffect

Here's how:

1. SETTLE IN. Initially, find a quiet space where you can sit, stand, or lie down, allowing yourself to be comfortable but awake. Set your intention to engage in this practice with the attitudes of a beginner's mind, seeing the breath as if for the first time. Use nonjudgment, knowing that the breath itself is neither good nor bad, and self-compassion, being kind to yourself, as this may not be an easy task.
2. LOCATE THE BREATH. While you're getting settled, start to become aware of where you notice the breath most prominently.

Everyone notices the breath in different places, sometimes at the tip of the nose, in the nostrils, the chest, or the belly, or possibly throughout the entire body. Zero in on where it is for you in this moment.

3. BREATHE IN, BREATHE OUT. As you breathe in, be aware that you're breathing in. You might notice the sensation of the breath as it comes in and goes out. Or if it helps with focus, you can say "In" to yourself when you're breathing in and "Out" as you're breathing out. As you do this, notice the spaces between the breaths.

4. SEE, TOUCH, GO. It's natural for your mind to wander. You may notice it sooner or later, but as soon as you do, you are in the now, you are in the space of awareness, a "choice point" where you have the opportunity to *see* where it has wandered to, work out the muscle of choice, *touch* it for a moment, and make the intentional decision to gently *go* back to the breath.

5. REPEAT. As Larry Rosenberg advised in *Breath by Breath: The Liberating Practice of Insight Meditation,* repeat these steps several billion times.

A quick note: Often when people engage in this practice, they become caught up with the notion that the goal or purpose is to keep the mind steady on the breath. That is not the purpose of what we're doing here. Instead, we're playing with our attention, setting the intention to be in the now and to be aware of the spaces where we have a choice to respond with "See, touch, go." So the very moment that you become aware of your mind wandering is a moment when you're in the now, in the space where there is choice, and it is of this choice point that we're trying to heighten our awareness. You might say that the more your mind wanders, the more choice points you get to notice, so it's all good. As we practice and repeat being aware of these spaces, we continue to prime our minds to recognize more choice in our daily lives and the fact that no matter how far we've strayed, we can always begin again.

How does "See, touch, go" work in your daily life?

- When you've been reading this book and integrating the practices and then notice that you've become caught up in living on automatic, *see, touch, go.*
- When you have a project to do and your mind wanders onto surfing the Web, *see, touch, go.*
- When you're trying to learn guitar and weeks have gone by where you haven't practiced, *see, touch, go.*
- When you swore you wouldn't yell at your child but find yourself reacting out of frustration, *see, touch, go.*

As you practice, release your expectations and be aware of your experience, nothing else. We are just getting started with the Now Effect.

6

NOW IS THE WAY

No valid plans for the future can be made by those who have
no capacity for living now. —ALAN WATTS

Pau was an aspiring young philosopher who spent his life in search of happiness. He read all the books he could get his hands on. From his home in Spain he journeyed across deserts, mountains, and oceans in search of teachers who could inspire in him the secrets to happiness. But although he touched moments of happiness, he was unable to sustain it for prolonged periods of time. Pau was disappointed and didn't know where else to search. One day he found himself on the doorstep of a Vietnamese Buddhist sage named Chogyam Nhat Zinn and conveyed his story of triumph and disappointment. Exhausted and depleted, Pau asked him, "Please, wise sage, what is the way to happiness?" Chogyam looked into Pau's eyes and told him, "Dear friend, your search is over, you have arrived, everything you need in order to find happiness is here right *now*." Pau felt confused and after a few minutes finally asked, "Okay, then, how do I get more of the *now?*" Chogyam waited a few moments, took a breath, smiled, and said, "Pau, there is no way to the now; now is the way."

As we move through the following pages, consider that there is no way to the now; now is the way. We don't need to try to get it because we already have it, it's right here. There is no more fundamental truth than this. As Jon Kabat-Zinn says, "This is it!"

In *The Power of Now: A Guide to Spiritual Enlightenment,* Eckhart Tolle spends much of the book making the case that time is a delusion of consciousness.

That said, we know that our brains are wired to use our past experiences as reference points to interpret the present moment and anticipate the future. This can pull us away from the moments of our lives.

Seeing now as the way means being comfortable in the paradox that there is nowhere to go but here but at the same time there's a need to change. There's nothing inherently mystical about putting intentional effort into being more present. It makes sense that the more attention you give to being present, the more likely your mind is inclined to move into the now.

Each time you drop into the spaces of your day and engage in them with mindfulness, you are watering the seeds of the Now Effect and allowing your mind to loosen its grip on being in the past or the future, making it clearer that now is the way.

As we end "Getting Started" and move into "Training Ground," take a minute to settle in and feel the connections of your body to the seat, bed, ground, or whatever else it is touching. Now, in this choice point, close your eyes and play with this practice, saying to yourself, "Breathing in, I am in the space, breathing out, I am in the now."

part II

TRAINING GROUND

The next series of chapters introduces you to the Training Ground of *The Now Effect*. Though they are all different, they have a unifying thread: helping you become more intimate with the spaces of your life and reconnect to what really matters.

The trick is to recognize where the spaces are in your daily life to stop and drop into a practice. A common obstacle to beginning is the belief that there has to be some special or perfect place to drop into the moments of our lives. The fifteenth-century mystical poet Kabir lays out the solution best: "Wherever you are, that is the entry point."

In other words, we can drop into the spaces of life any time we become aware of the now. It can happen while waiting on hold with the telephone company, standing in a line, stopping at a red light, sipping your coffee, arguing with your child, listening to a friend, surfing the Net at work, hearing your cell phone ring, standing in the shower, or even lying down in bed.

You can think of this section as a miniprogram within the book to get your feet wet as you drop these practices into the spaces of your life, again and again feeling into the Now Effect. Be playful with it. As you move through the training, you'll be priming your mind to notice the space between stimulus and response and the choice points all around you more spontaneously, inclining your mind toward the Now Effect.

Keep these five basic suggestions in mind:

1. WHEREVER YOU ARE, THAT IS THE ENTRY POINT. Keep this phrase in mind so that even in difficult moments you can be reminded of the way into the now.
2. LOOK FOR THE SPACES WITHIN THE PRACTICE. Just as we notice the spaces of awareness in our daily lives, we can also notice the spaces of choice in the practices themselves.
3. USE PLAYFUL DISCIPLINE. As you read and engage in the writings and practices of this book, set the intention to really devote yourself to it and bring the attitude of play.
4. PRACTICE "SEE, TOUCH, GO" WITH BEHAVIOR. Whenever you engage in any new practice, it's absolutely expected that you will fall off the wagon. There's no value in judging yourself for wandering off because it's a given; stressors and old habits arise and take us off track. Practice "See, touch, go." When you notice you haven't practiced for a while, *see* where you've gone off to, *touch* the moment, and gently *go* back to your intention of engaging with the Now Effect.

5. TREAT THIS AS AN EXPERIMENT. I suggest trying one of these practices throughout a single day before moving on to the next. After a time you can mix and match the practices, making them your own. It would be great to get a friend or partner to read this book with you so you can support each other. Treat this process as an experiment without expecting miracles. As soon as you expect some magical moment of enlightenment to occur, the mind sets up an internal monitor that searches for that and adds stress to what is naturally there. On top of that, any potential sign that the magic is not there opens the door for your attention to be diverted to doubt, which inevitably takes you away from the now.

SAY "YES!"

Jack Kent is a British author who tells a wonderful children's story of a young boy named Billy Bixbee who has a vivid imagination. One day Billy woke up and was surprised but curious to find a little dragon the size of a kitten in his room, and after petting him for a while, he enthusiastically went downstairs to tell his parents what he had found. As they laughed, his mom assured him, "Billy, there's no such thing as a dragon." As kids, we mostly believe what our parents tell us, and Billy did too, so he decided not to pay attention to or pet the dragon anymore. The next day Billy saw the dragon again, but it had doubled in size. When he went to his parents again, they gave him the same response. After a few days, the dragon continued to increase in size and was now taking up a majority of the space in their house. The parents started to notice that the house had moved and the father asked, "How did this happen?" Billy replied, "It was the dragon, who grew so big that he lifted the house and moved it!" "There's no such thing as dragons," his mom again told him. "There *is* a dragon!"

Billy insisted. As Billy reached down to pat the dragon's head, the dragon, being acknowledged, quickly shrank to a tiny size and the space in the house returned.

So it is with our lives. The old adage "What we resist persists" is too true. We say no to stress, no to fear, no to love, no to anger, no to connection. When a moment is met with "No!" a contraction occurs, walls are thrown up, and the body becomes tense, preparing to fight, flee, or freeze. The fact is, whenever you resist the pain that's there, your suffering increases.

As the pressure mounts, our mind builds up even more resistance and our chances of making change diminish. As strange as it may seem, a fundamental building block of creating change is learning how to say say "Yes!" to whatever feeling is here in this moment.

Saying "Yes!" creates a different experience. It fosters openness, warmth, spaciousness, and an awakening of our hearts and minds to our lives. Saying "Yes!" doesn't mean we want what is here or even that we like it, but it acknowledges the reality that it is here.

Tara Brach, the author of *Radical Acceptance,* suggests, "You just pause. Let go of thoughts and come into your body—notice what's going on. It's not saying yes to everything for the rest of your life. It's merely yes for this moment. Your heart relaxes and your mind opens."

now moment

Take a moment to consider who your dragons are. What feelings arise within you that you resist, sending the message of "No!"? Are they feelings of sadness, stress, anger, grief, fear, or maybe even joy?

To get a feel for this, think of a situation that happened in the last week that brought up a difficult feeling, such as anxiety, annoyance, or even shame. Maybe it was a conflict with someone at work, an argument with a loved one, the potential loss of someone close to you, or something you did that you feel bad about. Now let this scenario play through your mind like a movie reel and pause it at the moment of difficulty. Notice if there is a feeling or subtle thoughts of wanting to be anywhere else but here. That is the snap judgment of "No!" occurring. *This is the feeling of resistance.* When we can't accept the reality of the present moment and we fall into cycles of avoidance or escape, we add tension and stress and inevitably increase our suffering.

Consider what life would be like if you always walked around with thoughts and feelings of "No!"

Now practice tuning in to the feeling and saying "Yes!" This is a feeling of allowing, welcoming, and letting whatever is here be as it is. It sends the message internally that you are okay just the way you are.

What do you notice?

The fact is, whatever we practice and repeat becomes automatic. Habitually saying "No!" reinforces a belief that you are not okay and something is wrong with you. If you practice saying "Yes!" the message that is sent is you are okay just as you are, which leads to greater self-acceptance.

Throughout today, see if you can practice noticing when you're saying "No!" to a feeling that is here, and in that space of awareness, practice saying "Yes!" to the reality that is here and see what happens.

WHERE AM I STARTING FROM?

In any given moment, no matter what you're doing, three basic things are happening that make up your immediate experience: thoughts, emotions, and physical sensations. Whereas in the past many people believed the theory that the mind and body operate separately, a quick exercise can easily show us how our experience is linked in a triangle of awareness.

Here's the triangle in action:

Triangle of Awareness

Imagine you're walking to your car, which is parked at a meter, and from a distance you see a small envelope on your windshield. What do you experience first: thoughts, emotions, or physical sensations?

Some people might notice tension in their shoulders, while others are aware of the thought "That had better not be a ticket"; still another may feel worried or angry. Our brains are unique, so we may all experience different parts of the triangle first.

As stories begin to unfold in the mind about how terrible it would be if you got a ticket, your shoulders begin to tighten more, the pit in your stomach begins to grow, and anger or fear may rise. Memories flood in about all the times you got tickets before and how your bank account just shrank by $65. As the envelope starts to come into focus, the thought comes up, "I know it's a ticket, I just know it, why does this always happen to me?" Your breath and heartbeat become more rapid. As you approach the windshield and get closer, it actually looks as though the envelope is bigger than the ones tickets come in; your heartbeat slows down, and your anger and fear shift to confusion. As you grab the envelope and open it, you find a note from a friend saying "Just saw your car, hope you're well, thinking of you." Relief washes over your body and mind.

This triangular inner drama happens rapidly, beneath your awareness. As you bring understanding and attention to the experience of this triangle in action, you effectively create memories of it and alert your mind to be more aware of it. Since we know that the mind uses past memories as reference points to make judgment calls and decisions, the next time you walk to your car and see an envelope on the windshield, you are more likely to move out of the autopilot cycle and into a space of awareness where you can intentionally consider alternatives, practicing a more flexible mind, regulating your body, and developing more reliable intuition.

Just as with reading, walking, and riding a bike, it's all about practice.

As you practice, the understanding and memory of this triangle become a reference point that your subconscious relies on to perceive the world.

Let's face it, most of us have very busy days, even if our busyness is just in our minds, and now you can take an opportunity to drop into a space of being rather than doing and notice this triangle in action. One way to practice a mindful check-in is by asking yourself, "Where am I starting from right now?" This question invites your mind to mindfully check in with your body, emotions, and thoughts.

If you like more structure, you are welcome to experience the triangle in the following order:

1. BODY. Usually, underneath all the skewed stories of our minds, there is a straightforward physical feeling that arises in the body, telling us exactly what is going on. The problem is that we're trained to be up in our heads so much and are therefore so cut off from our bodies that we don't realize the wisdom our bodies hold. We can use our body as a barometer to let us know what's up and as a reminder to step into the spaces in our lives.

   Take a few moments to check in with your body. Notice your posture and any sensations such as heat, coolness, achiness, tension, tightness, heaviness, lightness, pain, or looseness. Notice if your energy feels right or depleted. If you don't notice any sensation, just notice that there is no sensation; that is fine. What is your body telling you?

2. EMOTIONS. Go ahead and check in with your emotions. Are you frustrated, calm, happy, sad, annoyed, restless, tired, scared, or joyful? See if you can put a name to how you're feeling emotionally. Get a sense for how it feels in your body. Frustration can often feel like tension, restlessness can feel as though your body wants to move, joy can feel like an expansion or looseness.

3. THOUGHTS. Just as we can sit back in a movie theater and watch the action on the screen, we can check in with our thoughts by being aware of what stories are being spun. They may be thoughts about the future or the past, judgments about the mindful check-in or this book in general, or maybe nonsensical thoughts and images.

Whatever you find during this mindful check-in, remember that the outcome is not that important. Instead, it is an opportunity to give your mind the experience of tapping into the triangle of awareness and watering the seeds of the Now Effect. As you do this, you can start to see just how often you live on automatic and that there are more choices about how to live in this world than you realized.

www.youtube.com/NowEffect

FEEL THE SPACES IN YOUR BODY

The sun was shining in through the window of a densely packed yoga studio, and the two people next to me were moaning through their poses. It wasn't something I was used to, and of course I became distracted by a barrage of automatic judgments—"Do they really need to do that?" and "That's really strange"—as I became restless and tense. Pretty quickly I was able to notice the triangle of awareness and came back to a mindful check-in, grounding myself to the now and redirecting my intention to be there with my body. The yoga instructor recited a quote from the thirteenth-century Sufi poet Rumi: "The body is a screen that reveals and partially hides the light that is blazing inside your presence." He instructed us to sit up straight and create an opening in the body so the light could shine through.

As I placed my hands behind me on the ground and began to gently open my chest, I repeated the words "Breathing in, opening my chest, breathing out, receiving what is here." The space that I created allowed the words "Thank you" to flow through. At that moment I felt as if I were reintroducing a long-lost part of me; it felt good. Then a thought arose in my mind: "All these people here, the moaners and the nonmoaners, are just like me, wanting to feel a sense of joy and freedom." In that moment, I felt free.

We know that there is a mind-body connection, so mindfully stretching our bodies in ways that cultivate openness not only connects us to our bodies but affects our minds and creates the openings necessary for greater clarity and well-being. *A flexible body can lead to a flexible mind.*

At the very least what we're doing here is watering the seeds of flexibility, openness, and playfulness. There's something that feels good about creating space in our bodies and allowing what is hidden to be revealed.

One practice that has exploded in popularity in the past twenty years is yoga. Yoga is a wonderful way to open the spaces of our bodies. In bringing mindfulness to yoga, we're not trying to get anywhere but simply to be where we are with this breath, this body, whether it is pleasant, unpleasant, or neutral. As our bodies begin to change with our practice, our minds, hearts, and the way we see life will follow.

now moment

Here are seven simple and gentle opening poses to try out right now or at some point during the day. Creating time for yourself to drop into your body and notice the spaces inside can also help incline your mind toward seeing the spaces outside. Practice this as a sequence, or pick one and practice it for a minute or two at work or at home. This is a generous act of self-care.

You can do the Receptive Pose in a standing or sitting position. Start by putting your hands together so that your palms are touching in front of your heart. Feel the connection between your hands and heart and take a few slow deep breaths, allowing your mind to recognize that you're entering into these gentle opening poses.

Bring both arms slowly up to the sky so the palms are facing each other and rise onto your toes. Feel the openings along the sides of your body and in your chest.

Decide what you want to invite into your life and what you want to let go of. This could come directly from what you reflected on in chapter 3, "Understanding What Really Motivates You." You may want to invite in greater peace, ease with your emotions, or self-love. You may want to let go of judgment, a busy mind, or self-blame.

As you breathe in, imagine your arms receiving what it is that you want; as you breathe out, imagine that you are letting go of what you want to leave.

Sky-to-Earth Pose

Interlace your fingers and turn your palms to face the sky. Bring your arms gently back as you look up toward the sky or ceiling, continuing to feel the sides of your body opening up. If you're able, go up on your tiptoes for a moment, reaching for what you want more of.

See it, touch it, it's real.

Palm Pose

From the Sky-to-Earth Pose on the previous page, slowly arch your body to the left, feeling the right side of your body opening up from your arms to your hips. Hold this pose, breathing into the spaces on the right side of the body that are opening up. As you breathe, you can lengthen a bit more with each exhalation.

Now slowly shift your body to the same position on the other side.

Sitting with Arms Behind Back Pose

Gently take a seat on the floor or a yoga mat and sit with your legs crossed. Looking straight ahead, place both hands on the floor behind you, palms facing the floor, opening up your chest and shoulders. Breathe into your chest and sense the area around your heart opening.

Pelvis-Opening Pose

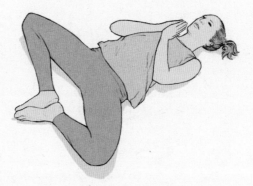

Lie back gently, placing both hands, palms together, on your heart. Bring your legs up so the soles of your feet are on the floor and your knees are pointing toward the ceiling. Allow both legs to fall slowly toward the floor, bringing the soles of your feet together. Sense and breathe into the openings in your hips. Without straining, allow each exhalation to guide your knees a bit closer to the floor and open the hips.

In some traditions this area of the body is known to represent some primitive emotions and is the storehouse of our sexuality. This pose can be enlivening, or it may be triggering if you've had past sexual trauma.

Please take this pose at your own pace, trusting your inner wisdom.

Open Twist Pose

As you lie on your back with both legs extended straight, bring your left knee up to your chest and, with your right hand, gently guide the knee over to the right side of your body. Either extend both arms straight out to the sides or extend your left arm and keep your right hand on the left knee. Turn your head slowly to look over your left arm, feeling into the openings up your spine and in your left hip.

Return to the midline with both legs extending straight out. Gently hug your right knee into your chest and repeat in the other direction, breathing into the openings and spaces that are there. When you're done, return to the resting position with both legs extended.

Child's Pose

The final pose in the sequence symbolizes safety and connection. Start off on your stomach and bring your knees underneath with your ankles close together. Bend forward from the waist until your chest is resting on your thighs and your head is touching the floor.

Extend both arms in front of your head and take a few deep breaths, feeling the openings on the sides of your body and your arms. Then move your arms beside your body and rest for a minute, acknowledging the gift of space you have given yourself.

10

IF YOU CAN NAME IT, YOU CAN TAME IT

We all get stuck; it's part of the human experience. Maybe we are continually distracted at work as projects mount, get hooked into the same arguments in our relationships, or just can't seem to get back on the treadmill. The prominence of this in our lives is the reason why so many of us look for help with getting unstuck.

In order to get unstuck, we need to remember that most of the way we react in this world is driven by our subconscious in the form of perceptions, judgments, and opinions that occur so quickly that we get stuck before we even have a chance. Our minds judge exercise as "bad" before the conscious excuse of being too tired or having no time emerges as a thought. Our partner was "wrong" the moment he opened his mouth. Without awareness of these snap judgments, the triangle of thoughts, physical sensations, and emotions erupts and we find ourselves stuck in a familiar pattern again and again.

In her book *Taking the Leap: Freeing Ourselves from Old Habits and Fears*, Pema Chödrön wrote, "Somebody says a harsh word and something in you tightens: instantly you're hooked. That tightness quickly spirals into blaming the person or denigrating yourself. The chain reaction of speaking and acting or obsessing happens fast."

However, there's a handy little phrase that I've adopted from my friend and colleague Dr. Daniel Siegel that can help us step out of our negative habitual cycles and into the now, a space of awareness where we can choose a different response: "If you can name it, you can tame it."

There's a second benefit to practicing this phrase. As you begin labeling what is actually happening in the present moment, you start becoming more aware of the factors that are driving you to be stuck. Your mind will then become primed to notice this feeling of being stuck, and over time it will become a trigger to move out of the cycle and into the now, giving you more clarity, possibility, and freedom.

now moment

Consider a recent moment when you felt stuck or got hooked into reacting in the same old ways that just don't work. Here is a four-step process to do right now to train your mind to get unstuck.

1. NAME THE STUCKNESS. Remember, "If you can name it, you can tame it." When you get stuck, say to yourself, "This is the feeling of being stuck."
2. FIND THE PHYSICAL SENSATION. Use your body as a barometer. Take a brief scan of your body, and become aware of where you notice the greatest sensation. Get a sense of how large it is, its shape, its color if any. Become curious about it. Becoming curious allows us to be playful and helps our minds break outside the box.

3. SEE CHOICES. Ask yourself the question "Is there another way I can see the situation I'm in? What choices do I have?" See if you can do this without judgment.
4. TAKE ACTION. Begin engaging in one of those choices.

If you find yourself feeling stuck today or anytime as you make your way through this book, practice these four steps to get unstuck and back onto the path of the Now Effect.

11

STOP

Our brains love to categorize and chunk information; it's a skillful way of retaining the barrage of data that comes our way. STOP is an acronym that I've adapted from the Mindfulness-Based Stress Reduction (MBSR) program and one of the most popular methods for helping the mind remember how to drop into and expand a space of awareness. The name of this one-minute practice stands for **S**top, **T**ake a breath, **O**bserve your body, emotions, and thoughts, and **P**roceed to what is most important.

Here are some examples of STOP in practice:

○ When you're at work, it's easy for your mind to wander off onto various engaging Web sites or software applications. When you notice this you can *stop, take a breath, observe what's happening, and then proceed with what really matters*, such as the project you're trying to get done.

○ Maybe you're about to fire off an angry text to your partner in

all caps after coming home to a sink full of dishes; this may
be a good time to bring in the STOP practice.
- ° Maybe you find your mind telling you stories about all the
work you have to do and how you'll never get it done in time;
use the STOP practice.
- ° Or maybe you're driving to work a few minutes late and someone
pulls in front of you, slowing you down; use the STOP practice.

Give yourself a minute to practice STOP right now
to get a feel for it.

Here it is:

www.youtube.com/NowEffect

S: Stop what you are doing.

T: Take a few deep breaths and then notice the breath as it is, as
you might when practicing "The breath as an anchor."

O: Observe your experience, similar to the way you would with
a mindful check-in.

P: Proceed by asking yourself the question "What is most important for me to pay attention to right now?"

What did you notice?

Now consider where the spaces are in your day where you can integrate STOP into your life. Then see if you can create reminders to
help you remember to practice in those moments. Put a sticky note
on your desk, type a reminder into your digital calendar, or get a
buddy so you can remind each other.

Remember, practicing this at times in the day that aren't hectic will help your mind remember to do it during more stressful moments. Though this practice may provide a side effect of helping you cool down and relax, that's not its true purpose. The purpose of STOP is to connect you with the space of this moment and the wisdom that lies within you.

12

GO

Stepping into the now doesn't happen only when we stop and pause our bodies; we can enter into a space simply by acknowledging what we're doing. There's no denying that we move, and there's no denying that movement is natural and healthy for us, so why not allow the movements of our lives to be the entry points into the now?

One of the most frequent movements that many of us engage in is walking. Like everything else in life, we learned, practiced, and repeated it for quite a while, and now it's automatic. What would happen if we brought some fresh eyes to the feeling of walking? Maybe we'd notice that we often walk with our head in front of our feet because we're so busy thinking. What would happen if we stood straight up, walked slightly slower, and tuned in to the environment all around us en route to our destination? Maybe we'd notice more pleasant sounds and sights and the feel of a gentle breeze or become aware that not everyone has the ability to walk, and gratitude might arise.

Exercise can also strengthen our brain, bolstering our ability to pay attention, retrieve information from long-term memory, think on our feet, and solve problems. The fact is, even if you just walk a few times a week, your brain benefits. Studies from all over the world show that your risk for dementia is cut in half when you engage in regular aerobic exercise. A twenty-minute walk twice a week will cut your risk of having a stroke in half. As you move, you also release three key neurotransmitters that support mental health: serotonin, dopamine, and norepinephrine.

So why not use exercise to practice becoming more present? When you are biking, know that you are biking; when you are running, notice what it's like to be running; when you are swimming, feel the water, notice the movement of your body; when you are stressed at the office, bring awareness to walking down the hallways and breathing.

now moment

When do you notice yourself moving in life? In between meetings at work, fitting in a trip to the grocery store, maybe even feverishly shooting off e-mail after e-mail? Pick one of those activities and begin to play with your attention, bringing awareness to the movements of your body. Maybe you can slightly slow down your walking to and from the car or down the hallway, or perhaps you can pause and do a few yoga poses in between e-mails. Try it out and notice how it changes your experience.

As you do this, know that you are training your mind to be here for your life. After you finish, practice expressing gratitude to your body for all that it does and see what happens next.

13

THE RED LIGHTS IN LIFE

Red lights are symbolic of all the moments in life when our minds want to go but we're told to stop or wait. You know exactly what I'm talking about here. We sit at a red light thinking, "When is this thing going to change? I'm late!" It often happens when we try to rush home to relax. Meanwhile, as we're hurrying up to wait, our body is getting tense and we're becoming more annoyed or anxious. By the time we get to where we want to be, we're stressed, so we're actually nowhere near where we want to be.

What's happening? The red light itself is a neutral event, but we subconsciously make a snap judgment that it is "bad" or "unfair." In that moment we're instantly hooked into a downward spiral. The muscles in the body tighten as anger or fear arises and a story follows in the mind about how terrible this moment is, the potential negative upcoming consequences of being late or how you always hit red lights and what bad karma you have. At the end of the day, we're often completely unaware of how such stories hijack our mind and body and go on to influence the many moments that follow.

What if, instead of obstacles, you thought of red lights as choice points, moments in time to choose a better way to relate to waiting? What if what followed was a choice to practice STOP or "The breath as an anchor" or do a brief mindful check-in when you noticed tension rising in the shoulders and decided to relax them?

The fact is that waiting is a part of life; it's how we choose to relate to it that makes all the difference.

I'm not suggesting that we reframe red lights as something good, because a red light itself is not inherently good or bad, it's just a light. But we want to intentionally try to see the times we spend waiting as a reminder that there are moments when we can come down from the stories in our minds and recognize that it isn't helping us to get worked up. When we drop into this space of awareness, we create the choice to respond differently.

As we do so, we continue to create new reference points of flexibility for the mind to draw from in the future, transforming instant, rigid reactions of getting hooked into more spontaneous, flexible responses.

now moment

Is there any time today when you can foresee yourself waiting? Are you going to be on hold, in a line, or maybe in the car at a red light? Try reminding yourself that those moments are choice points, and see if you notice your mind drop into a state of awareness. This may be a good time to practice STOP or "The breath as an anchor," or do a mindful check-in. Try it, and see what happens.

14

<hr />

A SPACE FOR MINDFUL EATING

There's a funny cartoon by Gary Larson of some cows eating grass in a green pasture with rolling hills. One cow's head is lifted up with eyes wide and a look of horror on its face. The caption reads, "Hey, wait a minute! This is grass! We've been eating grass!" Have you ever been sitting at a meal with someone or even by yourself and been halfway through without having tasted the food? If you're anything like me, the odds are highly likely that you've had this experience. Our minds are often somewhere else, worrying about where we need to be, watching television, or engrossed in conversation.

My first formal experience with mindfulness was through eating. I was challenged by a friend to really take my time and tune in to my senses while eating an orange. My mind told me that it was a silly exercise, but my friend encouraged me to have fun with it. So I began to look at the orange, taking in the color, the way the sun shined off of it, and all of its dimples. "That's interesting," my mind peeped out. I continued, and it turned out that not only did I see things in the orange I had never known were there before, such as the juicy membranes under the skin, but it was the best damn orange I had ever had in my entire life. Now, was it really the best orange, or was it the way I paid attention to it that made it so remarkable? I'll go with the latter.

The lack of intention and attention we bring to eating not only leads us to miss out on a potentially great meal but can also lead to making poor food choices and drive us to overeat as a way of coping with unacknowledged feelings and emotions. You may be in search of a "quick fix" that consists of caffeinated beverages and highly refined foods that burn quickly and spike your metabolism. Many people have learned to comfort and sedate themselves with food. Sadly, our "supersized" culture not only supports those tactics but capitalizes on them.

Since preparing and eating food are such essential components of our lives, why not recognize that this is a space that we can bring awareness to? Give yourself permission to slow down; there's nowhere to go, you've already arrived, take in the experience.

I had a client who suffered from stomach pains and was always complaining of a sensitive stomach. So I made a simple suggestion: that he slow down his eating slightly and chew a little more. When he tried this, he began to notice that his stomach didn't hurt quite as much because his food had been broken down prior to hitting his stomach.

I had another client who suffered from a food addiction and would often go to the bakery, buy a cake, and eat it that night. In session, we practiced mindful eating of a raisin in order to experience the concept of eating slightly more slowly and bringing all the senses to the food. To free herself from her regular snap judgments, she brought a beginner's mind to seeing it, touching it, smelling it, hearing it, and tasting it. She considered all the hard work it had taken many people to put this simple raisin in front of her that day, including her own efforts to gain the resources to pay for the session to learn the practice. In time, in combination with other work we did, she was able to slow down her eating and begin to eat smaller portions with a greater sense of appreciation of her food.

Another client with whom I did this practice said, "I've been downing raisins in handfuls my whole life, one after another. And it wasn't until now that I realized I don't even like raisins!" We both had a good laugh.

It's amazing what can happen when we drop into a space of awareness with something as seemingly routine as eating.

now moment

Consider the last few meals you've eaten. How often did you truly taste the food? Choose a snack or meal today, and tune in to the experience of eating. Slow down your eating slightly, and notice the sensations; contemplate all the natural elements (sun, rain, earth) that went into the formation of the food and all the human work (including yours) that was done to get the food to your table. This tends to naturally foster gratitude, which is an essential aspect of well-being. Chew a few more times before swallowing, knowing that making digestion easier is an act of kindness to your body.

Remember, though this practice may add pleasure and relaxation to enjoying your food, that's not its fundamental purpose. Instead, we're practicing this to incline the mind to be more aware of the spaces in life that allow us to choose healthier responses. As we do so, we are training the mind to be more flexible, compassionate, and present to the life we are living.

15

IT'S LIKE THIS . . . AND THIS TOO

Student: Elisha, sometimes I don't know what to do, I get
really frustrated.

Elisha: It's like this . . .

Student: Huh, I'm confused . . .

Elisha: And this too . . .

Student: I'm starting to get bored with your answers.

Elisha: It's like this.

Student: Now I'm restless.

Elisha: Ah, and this too . . .

Student: Ah . . .

There are so many subtle thoughts and feelings that sneak up on us and take us away from doing what we intend to do. In whatever endeavor you take on, you'll no doubt experience uncertainty, confusion, boredom, restlessness, or even frustration, which all have the effect of taking you away from your intention.

There are a couple of classic phrases that can change your perception of these feelings from a source of suffering to a source of support that helps bring your mind back to the now.

You guessed it: "It's like this . . ." and "And this too . . ."

"It's like this . . ." and "And this too . . ." basically say, "This is what is here right now," and bring us back to the present moment. Using those phrases will help shift you from choiceless reactivity to a choice point where you can regain control of the mind and come directly back to your intention.

now moment

Take a moment to close your eyes and take a few deep breaths. Open up to whatever is here and practice saying "It's like this . . ." or "And this too . . ."

Take this with you throughout the day and play with it. See if you can bring it in whenever you feel distracted, restless, bored, confused, or frustrated. Allow these phrases to return you to what really matters.

16

ONE MINUTE TO BRING
YOU INTO THE NOW

Now that you've worked through the Training Ground, you may have experienced more moments of dropping into the now. Here are ten more suggestions for how you might weave them into your daily life.

1. When you wake in the morning, before rushing off into your daily activities or checking your cell phone for messages, take a few deep breaths and check in with the sensations of your body. You may also practice "The breath as an anchor" and start the day from a grounded place.

2. As you take a shower, notice where you are. Are you in the shower or already at work? Take a few moments to come to your senses, smelling the soap, feeling the water against your skin, listening to the sounds of the shower, even watching the water as it splashes off your skin.

3. Think of one genuinely kind thing to say to one person in your house before leaving the home. If you live alone, notice a space where you can wish someone well.

4. Practice the Red Light Meditation at stoplights: Take a few deep breaths and soften your muscles if they're tense. Wish others on the road safe driving.

5. Practice "Go," walking to work or school slightly more slowly than usual and paying attention to the sensations of your body movement. Open your ears and listen for birdcalls and other sounds.

6. When you're at work or school, intentionally listen to colleagues when they speak to you. Instead of just hearing the words they're saying, notice their facial expression, the tone of their voice, and their body language. This will create a stronger connection.

7. At work or school, you can help your focus by putting up a small sign somewhere you can see it that reminds you to be present. You can write, "Breathing in, I am here, breathing out, I refocus on what's most important."

8. Before leaving work or school, take a moment to look back on the day and note the work that you were proud of and perhaps some things you could do better next time.

9. Before leaving your car to step into the house, practice a mindful check-in and inquire, "Where am I starting this moment from?" Consider how you want to be the rest of the evening. If there is family or a roommate at home, how would you like to be with them; if it's just yourself, what would you like the evening to look like?

10. As you lay your head on the pillow at night, consider, "Where was the good today?" If you are spiritual or religious, you might consider asking, "Where in this day did I notice God?"

Make a commitment to drop these practices into the spaces of your life and see what happens.

part III

KNOW YOUR MIND, CHANGE YOUR BRAIN

A number of years ago at Harvard, a group of researchers conducted an interesting study in which they had
volunteers learn a simple exercise on a piano keyboard and
practice it for an hour a day for five days a week, measur-
ing any change in the motor area of their brain, which
controls the movement of the fingers. As you may have sus-
pected, they found that there was growth in that area of the

brain. But there was another discovery. They had a different group look at the music and practice by imagining and thinking about doing the exercise for an hour a day for five days a week, and they found the same level of growth in the motor area of the brain. In other words, there was physical evidence that both the way we think and how we think have an influence on how our brain grows. This is called "neuroplasticity," *neuro* meaning the brain, *plasticity* meaning the ability to change.

The problem is, most of the time we don't know what we're thinking. The brain is passive, processing information coming in from our internal and external environments, and without awareness we can't actively manage the internal process of energy and information flow that we'll call mind. When we're habitually worrying about the future or rehashing the past, we are influencing the wiring of our brains to do that more automatically. When we consistently criticize ourselves or tell ourselves, "I'm not worthy," "Life will never get better," or "I can't do that," we change our brains in that direction.

Knowing the way you think and where you place your energy allows you to step away from the various stories and mind traps that don't serve you and enter the space of awareness where you can consider alternatives for creating a more flexible, healthier mind. In this section you'll come to understand that thoughts aren't facts and you can actually choose to water the seeds that are more supportive, rewriting the movie in your mind that may have kept you stuck for so many years. As you do so, you'll actually be rewiring your brain and changing the way you think *before* you think.

This is what the Now Effect offers: breaking free from past conditioning so we can live the life we want to.

17

THE MOVIE IN YOUR MIND

When I let go of what I am, I become what I might be.

—LAO TZU

In the summer of 2008 Congressman Tim Ryan of Ohio was feeling the accumulation of a relentless, nonstop work schedule and was heading toward burnout. Tim was thirty-seven years old, dressing the part of a politician in conservative suits, and on call at all times. He was living in two places, constantly traveling between Ohio and Washington, DC. All the moments of his life were accounted for. Tim loved his work, but he knew if he didn't change something soon, it wasn't going to last. His stress level was too high, and his mind was incessantly running with stories about what he could have done better in the past and what he needed to do in the future.

He found a weeklong retreat led by Jon Kabat-Zinn called "The Power of Mindfulness," which catered to leaders in their respective fields. Tim showed up in his suit and reluctantly checked in his two BlackBerrys. About three days into the retreat he was led into thirty-six hours of silence with the purpose of practicing stepping into the space of his life as it was. Somewhere within those thirty-six hours, he told me, "I started to realize that I was not my thoughts. I had read about this in books, but for the first time I was actually experiencing a separation between my awareness and the thoughts that were running through my head. I saw the same movie playing over and over again, but I wasn't participating, just watching. As I continued to do this, for the first time in a long time my body began to relax and my head loosened up. I felt like everything was going to be okay."

There's no question that our minds are the ultimate storytellers. They tell us who we are, what we can accomplish, what's to be feared, who's to be accepted, and ultimately what we believe.

Whatever we believe influences the way we think before we think, guiding those sneaky snap judgments that make up how we see the world and our every interaction. If we believe we can't give a speech, lose weight, or live without our smart phones, doing those things is going to be a lot harder, if not impossible. The same goes for getting through the difficult moments in life, whether a relationship conflict or working through stress, anxiety, depression, or addiction.

Though no one really knows when beliefs begin to form, we do know that from the time we're in the womb we're already sensing the environment around us, taking in and processing information. We also know that from the moment we're born our brains start to wire in what is good and bad, right and wrong, fair and unfair from our parents, religious institutions, and the media.

There's a difference between thinking and knowing that you're thinking. The latter implies having an awareness of a space between the knower (you) and the thought. The fact is, you are not your thoughts, and you don't need to be enslaved by them.

Noticing the unhealthy habitual patterns of the mind has enormous power, as it stretches the space between our awareness and the thoughts themselves. You can say, "My mind is circling that bad neighborhood again," and in that space of awareness you can redirect the energy of your mind down another road. As you practice knowing your mind, you'll begin to understand that you don't have to identify so strongly with old beliefs or unhealthy stories and can increase your sense of distance from them.

now moment

Take a minute or so to close your eyes, get a sense of your body as it is, and imagine that you are sitting in a dark movie theater looking at the images and listening to the dialogue on the screen of your mind. While you are doing this, there's no need to create thoughts or try to change any of them; just sit back and be aware of what's there. Are there many thoughts or few? You might notice a dialogue, the thoughts we hear such as "I need to go to the grocery store," "Why am I doing this practice? I have other things to do," or "I wonder when the economy is going to pick up?" Or maybe you notice images or pictures. Check to see if you notice more dialogue or images or an equal combination of the two. As you close your eyes, see if you can notice the spaces between the thoughts themselves. Go ahead, take a few moments and give it a shot.

www.youtube.com/NowEffect

This Now Moment gives you the experience of relating *to* your thoughts instead of *from* your thoughts. As you practice, you'll begin to recognize the space between your awareness and your thoughts, which will help you see that thoughts are simply mental events that come and go and you don't need to be enslaved by them.

18

REWRITE THE MOVIE IN YOUR MIND

If you correct your mind, the rest of your life will fall into place.
　　　　　　　　　　　　　　　　　　　—LAO TZU

The narrative you hold about your life can contain some very limiting beliefs that keep you stuck. The good news is that you have the ability to rewrite your life story, starting today. I'm not talking about rewriting the facts, such as having abusive parents or perfect parents or being bullied at school. What I am talking about is how you've interpreted those facts and created a story about your life that may not be accurate or helpful in your present situation.

The day my parents told my sisters and me they were getting divorced, as most kids do, I took it upon my shoulders and planted a deep seed that their divorce was my fault and I was therefore unworthy of love. Because the divorce happened long ago, the belief slipped into my subconscious. It wasn't something that was readily accessible to me, yet it influenced how I felt about myself and my intimate relationships. I formed a shell around my heart, and sometimes when someone tried to get in, the belief would shut me down and cause me to retreat further into that shell.

It wasn't until I was an adult that I was able to expose the belief and become aware that I was the one who had created that story. I could understand that the divorce wasn't my fault. I realized that I am loved, and I felt the enclosure around my heart open and a flood of grief, love, and awe pour out.

now moment

We can dismantle our unhealthy stories and weave new ones. Try the following:

1. EXPOSE THE BELIEF. The first thing you need to do is to look back into your history and see if there are any experiences you may have given meaning to that translated into a limiting belief. Are you holding on to a deep thought that you are unworthy, unlovable, or incapable in some way? Do you believe that you can't do certain things or you'll never accomplish others? Can you accept the reality that those beliefs and feelings are there? See if you can find the courage within to call them out, label them, write them down, and expose them. As you expose your beliefs, a space widens between your awareness and the thought or belief. This space is another "choice point" where you can choose to come down from your thoughts and into the direct experience of your emotions.

2. FEEL INTO THE EMOTIONAL REACTION. The belief is strong and instantaneous because it has been programmed into deep emo-

tional regions of your brain. You need to find the emotion that is tied to this belief so you can begin to work with it. Is it fear, anger, guilt, shame, or another feeling? Where is it in your body? See if you can get a sense of the texture of the emotion as it manifests in the body. Does it come out as tightness, heaviness, tension, or another feeling? We need to acknowledge the reality of this feeling and give it space. We can then choose to relate to it differently, with compassion.

3. RELATE TO EMOTION WITH COMPASSION. It's not enough to expose the emotion; we need to relate to it in a way that is restorative and healing. The way to do this is to get in touch with the part of yourself that exudes kindness, compassion, and/or love. You can think of it as a voice inside that wants to help. As you dip your attention into the physical presence of the emotion, see if you can hold it with awareness. Imagine cradling it as you would a small baby. If this is difficult, imagine someone you know, living or dead, who symbolizes a wise and compassionate awareness, and imagine that person giving you comfort as you allow that feeling to flow through you. If any judgments arise around this step (for example, "This is so Pollyanna" or "I can't do this"), *see, touch, go,* noticing those thoughts as mental events, and come back to this practice. From your new relationship with the feeling, you can begin to rewrite the story.

4. REWRITE THE STORY. My client Julie was told her entire life by her parents that she wasn't a good writer and she should come to accept the fact, thus staving off any future disappointment. It was only when she was in college that she started receiving positive feedback about her writing. However, she couldn't accept the praise until she realized that "being a bad writer" was an old story and a new one was starting to develop. She said to

herself, "In the past I have had difficulty with my writing due to my old story; this story is not a fact, and moving forward, I'm going to open up to the new possibility that I am indeed a good writer." We turned this into a practice: on an inhalation Julie acknowledged the limiting belief that she wasn't a good writer, and on an exhalation she let go of her old limiting belief and opened to new possibilities.

Whatever your limiting beliefs are, they've likely been repeated in your mind over and over again so that this limiting story is deeply ingrained and automatic. It can take some time to shake an old story and retrain your brain, so don't go into this practice expecting immediate results; think of it as an experiment. Remember, you're planting seeds for a new story, and it may take some time for it to take root. Be patient as your mind develops new neural connections that will soon begin to tell a new story of hope, ease, and success.

Practice "Breathing in, I see my limiting belief, breathing out, I let it go and open to new possibilities."

19

MEMORY MATTERS

When you place enough attention on any one thing, your mind becomes subconsciously primed to see the world through that lens. Where you choose to place your attention has an effect on the memories that are created in your mind. Every experience you have is stored as a memory to serve as a reference point for your mind to interpret the present and anticipate the future. It influences your underlying thoughts, images, dreams, and perceptions. This conditioning begins early on in life and continues through adulthood. If our perception of reality is influenced by what we spend our time paying attention to from moment to moment, it's a good idea to look at what's influencing our thoughts and the way we see the world.

We spend an enormous amount of attention on all kinds of things in our daily life. According to the Nielsen Company, the average American watches more than four hours of television per day. Is the attention we spend on television priming our minds to see life as an unfolding drama? Does a hyperfocus on Facebook and Twitter make interactions with friends, family, and colleagues just another status update? Are online matchmaking sites turning people into objects or commodities?

How about the amount of attention we give to worrying about the future or the past? It doesn't seem too far-fetched to think that this would cause a worried or depressed perspective on the unfolding moments of our lives. For decades researchers have been finding that practicing and repeating a simple exercise can influence our underlying thoughts and that those thoughts can lead us to believe and act as though we are old or young, smart or dumb, secure or insecure.

The question is, can we intentionally create experiences and memories that work for us? Congressman Tim Ryan said that after practicing becoming more present to the moments of his life, he began to become more present with his constituents. As we practice and repeat seeing the spaces between our awareness and our thoughts, we begin to experience fewer moments of getting hooked into "what-ifs" and "what-could-have-beens."

Tim Ryan's experience is not unique, and there is nothing mysterious about this process; it's how our minds work. The mind relies on memories to determine how we perceive and react to events in our lives. In other words, *memory matters*. The very moment we recognize that a past memory is impacting our perception of the present moment or how we're anticipating the future, we have stepped outside of it, created a space, and broken free from it. On the flip side, the practices you have been engaging in throughout this book have already begun working on your subconscious cognition, creating new, mindful memories that will eventually change your underlying thoughts for the better, inclining your mind toward the Now Effect.

Ask yourself how what you pay attention to plays a role in how you perceive your life. Do you routinely engage in anxious thinking, depressed thinking, flexible thinking, pessimistic thinking, or optimistic thinking? How does this automatic way of perceiving the world affect how you are with your family, your job, your relationships, and yourself? How does it affect the way you relate to your stress and pain? How do you want your memories to work for you?

20

THOUGHTS ARE NOT FACTS

Your worst enemy cannot harm you as much as your own
unguarded thoughts.   —BUDDHA

Imagine that today is not your day. You woke up in the morning feeling anxious but didn't know why. You burnt your toast, you couldn't find any decent music to listen to, and as you looked down you noticed a stain on your pants. When you finally arrived at work, you were greeted by a mountain of projects on your desk. Your boss came up to you and asked, "What's wrong with you today?" and left before waiting for an answer.

It's midday, and as you're waiting in the hallway, your mind spins about how it's been a pretty crummy day and life just doesn't seem to be moving in the direction you'd like it to. A colleague walks toward you, and although you raise your hand to wave hello, the person just looks at you and continues to walk by.

What is the first thought that crosses your mind about that colleague? Consider the triangle of awareness. What was the emotion (for example, frustration, concern, or shame) and how was your body feeling?

Under such circumstances, many people experience various thoughts that are connected with uncomfortable emotions:

○ "What did I do wrong?"
○ "I'm worthless."
○ "I knew it, nobody likes me."
○ "Why does this always happen to me?"
○ "What's the point, really?"

Okay, now shake that one off. Here's a new scenario:

Let's say your day started off great. You drove through all green lights on the way to work, and upon arriving your boss told you what a fantastic job you've been doing and how she's going to give you a 15 percent raise and an extra week of vacation. As your mind is spinning around all the ways this will enhance your life, a colleague walks down the hall toward you, and as you lift your hand to say hello, she just walks by.

Now what comes up in your mind? Many people might have an alternative viewpoint here.

○ "I wonder what's wrong with her?"
○ "I hope she's okay."
○ "Maybe she didn't see me."
○ "Oh well, who cares."

The exact same event was interpreted differently because of different precipitating events and moods.

The bottom line: thoughts aren't facts; they are mental events that pop up in the mind and are dependent on our mood, attitude, and beliefs.

Interpreting events based on these factors happens all the time.

If we know we're walking into work with our mind inclined toward frustration or stress, we can become more aware of our initial thoughts, get some space from them, and bring an unbiased perspective to our interactions with others.

The fact is, we don't need to believe everything we think.

Knowing how our minds can be primed and that our thoughts are not facts can give us mastery over the habitual tendencies of our minds.

now moment

Take this opportunity to reflect on a recent event where your mind jumped to a conclusion. How did it get there? Did your mood have anything to do with it? What would have been different if your mood had been flipped 180 degrees? Next time you become aware of your mind jumping to a conclusion, recognize that in that very moment you have created a little distance from the thought itself, and in this space you'll find a choice point and can choose to remind yourself that thoughts are not facts. If you're feeling imbalanced, you might bring in a daily building block, such as STOP, mindful check-in, or "The breath as an anchor," to get centered and then reflect on where your head was at the time. You may discover how you came to that autopilot interpretation, and the reality check will help you in future interactions.

TOP TEN HIT LIST

I n Mindfulness-Based Cognitive Therapy (MBCT), an eight-week group program that Zindel Segal, PhD, and his colleagues initially created to help people not relapse back into depression, we suggest that people create a Top Ten Hit List of their most automatic negative thoughts (ANTs).

Creating a Top Ten Hit List of the ANTs that run around in your head is a playful way to approach those difficult thoughts. When they're captured on paper, you can't help but see the space between your awareness of the thoughts and the thoughts themselves, which allows you to gain freedom from them. As you review your list, you can begin to take these "facts" not so seriously.

To help you create your list, here are some common negative thoughts adapted from those of researchers Steven Hollon and Philip Kendall. See if you identify with any of them.

Automatic Negative Thoughts = ANTs
1. I feel as though I'm up against the world.
2. I'm no good.

3. Why can't I ever succeed?

4. No one understands me.

5. I've let people down.

6. I don't think I can go on.

7. I wish I were a better person.

8. I'm so weak.

9. My life's not going the way I want it to.

10. I'm so disappointed in myself.

11. Nothing feels good anymore.

12. I can't stand this anymore.

13. I can't get started.

14. What's wrong with me?

15. I wish I were somewhere else.

16. I can't get things together.

17. I hate myself.

18. I'm worthless.

19. I wish I could just disappear.

20. What's the matter with me?

21. I'm a loser.

22. My life is a mess.

23. I'm a failure.

24. I'll never make it.

25. I feel so helpless.

26. Something has to change.

27. There must be something wrong with me.

28. My future is bleak.

29. It's just not worth it.

30. I can't finish anything.

More often than not, these thoughts occur less frequently and are much less convincing and believable when we're feeling well and things seem to be going our way.

What is on your Top Ten Hit List? On a sheet of paper write down your top ANTs. Do you notice the ANTs popping up more when you're alone, at work, with friends, or with family? Throughout your day, when you become aware of the thoughts, remind yourself that you're in a space of awareness and can gain perspective and bring your attention back to what is most important in that moment. You can do this over and over again, bringing a sense of compassion and kindness toward yourself during this process.

YOUR MIND TRAPS

We cannot solve our problems with the same thinking we used when we created them. —ALBERT EINSTEIN

Portia Nelson wrote a poem called "Autobiography in 5 Short Chapters" that speaks to the learning that naturally happens when we work to become more aware of the mind traps that enslave us.

Before you read over the following, allow your mind to settle in and be present to this space in time. Practice "Breathing in, I am here, breathing out, I am now." If your mind wants to speed through the poem, practice "See, touch, go" and then continue.

Chapter I
I walk down the street.
There is a deep hole in the sidewalk.
I fall in.
I am lost . . . I am helpless.

It isn't my fault.
It takes forever to find a way out.

Chapter II
I walk down the same street.
There is a deep hole in the sidewalk.
I pretend I don't see it.
I fall in again.
I can't believe I am in the same place.
But it isn't my fault.
It still takes a long time to get out.

Chapter III
I walk down the same street.
There is a deep hole in the sidewalk.
I see it is there.
I still fall in . . . it's a habit.
My eyes are open.
I know where I am.
It is my fault.
I get out immediately.

Chapter IV
I walk down the same street.
There is a deep hole in the sidewalk.
I walk around it.

Chapter V
I walk down another street.

Becoming aware of and breaking free from our mind traps follows the same progression. You can think of mind traps as categories of automatic negative thoughts (ANTs) or stories we get caught in that inevitably trap us into unhealthy patterns of reactivity and keep us blind to the spaces of awareness that offer the choice to respond differently.

Look at the list of mind traps below and see if you identify with any of them.

- CATASTROPHIZING. This style of thinking expects disaster, assumes the worst, and amplifies anxiety. You automatically imagine the worst possible thing that could happen in any situation or challenge you face. Your mind goes on and on about what-ifs until it reaches the worst-case scenario. For example, when your boss says you're behind on your reports, your mind snowballs from this statement to losing your job and having difficulty putting food on the table.

- EXAGGERATING NEGATIVE DETAILS AND DISCOUNTING THE POSITIVE. These mind traps go hand in hand and contribute to distraction and depression. You reject all positive experiences, insisting that they don't count, and magnify the negative details. You may say something positive, then say the word "but," and then say something negative. For example, "It was good that my boss liked my presentation, but not everyone clapped as usual when I was finished." This gives more power to the negative. It would be more accurate to replace the *but* with *and*, giving both statements equal weight.

- MIND READING. This is another mind trap that can lead to increased stress and anxiety. Without actual evidence or information about what people are thinking or how they are feeling, you convince yourself that you actually know what they are thinking and feeling and why they are acting the way they do. If a friend does not return your call, you may think he is angry with you when there may be many reasons why—and they may have nothing to do with you. These unfounded and most likely inaccurate interpretations tend to keep you unnecessarily anxious, agitated, or depressed, which makes it more difficult to be in the here and now.

○ SUFFERING FROM "THE SHOULDS." This is a common mind trap that can lead to stress along with anger or guilt. If you suffer from "the Shoulds," you have a list of unbreakable rules. If others break them, you get angry, and if you break them, you feel guilty. While you have been reading this book a thought may have arisen that you "should" be more diligent with any suggested practices. Beating yourself up for not following a self-imposed "should" can keep you stuck in a pattern of frustration and resentment that will lead you to put down this book entirely. Paradoxically, "the Shoulds" can often keep you from doing what you want or need to do.

○ BLAMING. This is another mind trap that can strip you of your power to make a change for the better. You either hold others responsible for your own shortcomings or blame yourself for others' problems. Either way, blame takes you away from knowing and doing what is most important right now.

You might not be aware of these mind traps happening or notice how you get stuck in them. You may catastrophize because you think, "That's just who I am." When you become aware of them, you can get a bit of perspective on them and realize that there's another way to see situations, but you may still get stuck in them.

Eventually, as you practice acknowledging your mind traps, you'll notice more often when the mind catastrophizes, drop into the space between stimulus and response, and shift your attention so you don't get caught in the snowball reaction. Finally, with awareness and practice, your perspective will begin to shift as you become able to anticipate mind traps before you are drawn into them and choose a different path.

23

THE INEFFECTIVE ART OF BLAMING

Though blaming is a mind trap, it deserves more attention as it is one of the most destructive habitual ways we have of relating to ourselves and others.

When I was a kid, my family went on a ski trip to Mammoth Mountain, California. I felt like I was pretty good and told my dad that I was ready to go on a harder run. So up we went. My body was becoming increasingly filled with nervous and excited energy as I saw the lift passing the usual stops and approaching the end of our ride. I performed a flawless exit from the lift, and as you can imagine, I was extremely proud of myself. I took off down the hill ahead of my dad and soon noticed that there were a number of moguls (small bumps in the snow). I started going faster. I then hit the moment that anyone who has skied or snowboarded experiences where you feel out of control; fear surged through me as my legs became wobbly, and I smashed into the snow face-first. When my dad came up to where I was lying in the snow, the first words out of my mouth were "Dad, it's your fault!"

Though that story usually leaves a few people chuckling around the dinner table and may have been age-appropriate behavior for a kid, when an adult blames others frequently, it isn't quite as funny.

Blaming isn't a conscious act; it happens automatically and habitually. We learn it from our parents, teachers, cultures, and religions. As children, when we feel we are in trouble, our sense of belonging or love from others feels threatened, so we practice and repeat the art of blaming so we can deflect threats away from ourselves.

After enough repetitions, of course, blaming becomes automatic and slips beneath our conscious radar, and we no longer think about it; it's just the way we're programmed. Half the time (or more), we don't even notice we're doing it. Blaming is commonplace.

I frequently see blaming in action in couples therapy, from proclamations as blatant as "It's all your fault. All our problems are because of you" to "You make me nuts when you don't put the toilet seat down." Individuals often engage in the self-blame game. We say, "There's just something wrong with me." Self-blame is sometimes the most insidious and needs to be recognized and addressed. I also see blame in the workplace: "The reason I didn't get my work done was because my coworker kept distracting me." Or with addictive behaviors: "If I didn't have so many friends around me who drank, I wouldn't be drinking as much." Whether it's self-blame or blaming others, blaming is an unhealthy mind trap. Although it may give us short-term relief, it always comes back to bite us and makes us feel worse.

Identifying blaming as a mind trap allows us to name it, step into the choice point, and get unhooked. Naming the blame allows us to see the anger that's driving it. In a space of awareness we can notice the burning in our chest, the constriction of our hands. We can play with bringing compassionate attention to the feeling and begin to have some insight into what we truly need, which is usually more self-compassion. Identifying blaming and moving on from it reinforces what you learned earlier: "If you can name it, you can tame it."

Recognize if there is anyone you are blaming right now, including yourself, or maybe you can recall a recent experience when you blamed someone. Sit and breathe for a moment so you can check in to see what emotion exists behind that mind trap. Whether the feeling is anger, grief, sadness, or fear, try understanding how it arises in your body and allow it to be there, exploring the physical feeling and the emotion with kind attention and a beginner's mind. Notice any judgments you attach to feeling vulnerable. Be with the experience. Trust in your deep strength to be able to be with what you are experiencing.

24

NOW ON YOUR DIET

*It isn't what happens to us that causes us to suffer; it's what
we say to ourselves about what happens.*

—PEMA CHÖDRÖN

Georgia was a client of mine who suffered from food addiction
and an endless cycle of yo-yo dieting. Every month, it seemed,
she started a new weight-loss wonder diet that would "fix" all her
problems. The more diets she went on, the more her mind would
swim with desires or cravings for food. Sooner or later she would
roll by the bakery and think, "I've been really good lately, just a little
treat would be okay." There's nothing inherently wrong with this, but
before she knew it, she would find herself at home halfway done with
a small cake. Then the ANTs would arise: "Nothing's ever going to
change, I've tried every diet, no one can help me, what's the use?"
The greatest travesty in this is that most of the time she ate so fast she
never really tasted or enjoyed the cake.

As we've come to understand, our minds are constantly subconsciously making decisions about what we're going to do next. Have you ever found yourself feeling nervous energy, and then, all of a sudden, you're searching for a "quick fix" that consists of caffeinated beverages or highly refined foods that burn quickly and spike your metabolism? Though this response seemed automatic, your mind made the decision that it was what you needed in that moment. Many people have learned to calm their anxious or depressed minds with food.

When we change the way our minds relate to food, new doors open and the possibilities unfold.

When I talked about it with Georgia, she was full of mind traps. She told me that at times she would minimize the issue by saying to herself, "I only ate half the cake, usually I eat the entire thing." Other times she would blame others for her behavior, saying, "You would overeat too if you were married to him." And still she would find herself in front of the bakery, bargaining and cutting deals with herself: "I'll start paying attention to what I'm eating after this next big meeting." Even after she gave in to her urges she would practice all-or-nothing thinking: "I can't believe I just ate that, I'm a terrible person, my whole diet is ruined."

Because she had practiced and repeated this type of thinking over time, she wasn't even aware that it was happening. To help her see the space between her mind and her mind traps, I had her create a card of the mind traps that she kept in her pocket as a shortcut to weight loss. Every time she walked in front of a bakery, she pulled out the card and looked to see if any of the mind traps were in play. This brought her out of her mind and into a space of awareness, a choice point, allowing her the freedom to choose a different response.

What was the different response?

She chose to bring in a short practice such as STOP, mindful check-in, or "The breath as an anchor" to come down from her anxious mind and into the now. She continued by locating where the feeling was in her body so she could say "Yes!" to the feeling that was there and ride the urge, the physical sensation, that was tugging her to eat. In a short time, the tension in her chest appeared, rose, peaked, and then began to decrease. Over time, this helped give her mind the experience to draw upon that she doesn't need to react by giving in to the urge.

She also developed a ritual of setting the intention to bring mindfulness to eating before she ate a meal. She considered all the hard work it had taken many people to put the food in front of her, including her own efforts to pay for and prepare the food. She ate slightly more slowly than usual and allowed her mouth the luxury of tasting the food she was eating. This helped her eat less and enjoy her food more.

Georgia now sees her relationship to food as another way to bring her into the now. She eventually joined a mindful eating group online and developed a regular exercise routine, and though she's relapsed a couple times, she doesn't judge herself as much. She has also lost weight and kept it off and for once feels more in control of her life.

Becoming aware of these common weight-loss mind traps can give us the edge of not only a healthier mind but a healthier body.

now moment

You've already practiced bringing mindfulness to eating a snack or meal. If you struggle with food, think of the last time you gave in and consider which of the mind traps came into play. Are there certain types of food that particularly make you weak in the knees? Right now, take a little card and write the mind traps you identify with on that card. In the coming weeks, practice these four steps for a shortcut to weight loss.

1. Name the mind trap.
2. Practice grounding to the now.
3. Ride the urge in the body as it rises and falls.
4. When you eat, set the intention to eat mindfully.

Each time you practice and repeat this, you will sow the seeds of greater freedom.

25

MAYBE SO, MAYBE NOT

There is a story of a wise old man who lived in the long-lost village of Andechelm. Everyone in the village looked up to him and sought his advice. One summer day, a villager came to him in a state of panic. "Wise sage, I don't know what to do; my oxen have escaped and now I am unable to plow my fields. This is dreadful! This must be the most terrible thing that could ever happen!" The sage looked him in the eye and replied, "Maybe so, maybe not." Bewildered, the man went back to his family and told them that the sage was no sage after all and was one card short of a full deck because surely this was the most terrible thing that could ever have happened.

The next morning, unable to plow his fields, the man took a hike over the hills and in the distance saw a number of horses grazing in the field. Immediately he ran back and got his son to help him catch the horses. Surely this would alleviate his troubles. With a bit of effort, they brought the horses back, and the man realized how blessed he was; plowing was even easier than before. He remembered the sage and felt so embarrassed that he ran over to him to apologize. As soon as he laid eyes on the sage, he mumbled, "Please accept my apologies, you were absolutely right. If I had not lost my oxen, I wouldn't have gone on that walk and would never have captured those horses. Now, you must admit, this is the most wonderful thing that could ever happen." The old sage looked into the man's eyes and said, "Maybe so, maybe not."

"Is this guy a joke?" thought the man. "I vow never to come to him again." The man returned home to his family. A few days later, while his son was trying to tame the horses, he was bucked off and broke his leg and was now unable to help out with the farm. The farmer needed his son and was devastated. "This is the most terrible thing that could have happened," he thought. "How will we eat?" Against his previous vow, the farmer went to the sage and told him what had happened. "You must see the future. How did you know this would happen? This is a great time of struggle, this time you must agree with me, this is the most terrible thing that ever happened." Once again the sage, calmly and with compassion, looked into the farmer's eyes and replied, "Maybe so, maybe not." The farmer was enraged by this response and stormed back to the village.

The very next day the king's troops came into the village, looking for all young men who were healthy and able to fight in the new war. Because of his injury, the villager's son was the only young man not taken to fight in an impossible war where almost all the men would surely die.

What we think is a negative event may be the seed of something positive. Does getting a speeding ticket mean the police are out to get you, or is it a reminder to slow down so you don't get into an accident? When someone doesn't call you back does that mean he's angry with you or simply that he's busy? Our default reaction is to go to the story in our minds that puts a negative light on any interaction. We get so caught up in our mental stories that we fail to see the wisdom of the sage. When we are aware enough to notice a story unraveling, we are present in a space of awareness and can be mindful of it, giving ourselves the ability to consider alternative stories or to get in touch with a greater truth.

now moment

Be on the lookout for your mind automatically labeling events as negative. Experiment with saying "Maybe so, maybe not" when your impulse is to see something in the worst possible light.

When you ask yourself, "Is there another way I can see this?" you may be surprised by what you find.

26

NOW AT WORK

John believed he was the best multitasker and hardest-working person in the human resources department of a large corporation. Day after day he worked hard, juggling many tasks at once, and it seemed that his in-basket was never empty. But he had been there for eighteen months and had never received a raise. Recently, during his workday, his mind felt more cluttered than ever as thoughts of "It shouldn't be this hard" kept racing around his mind. As the stress mounted, he began to get stomach pains and became increasingly distracted from his priorities and easily swayed toward less important tasks, such as checking his e-mail and surfing the Web. Because the quality of his work was slipping, his mind began to snowball into catastrophic thinking about getting fired, having difficulty finding new work, and not having money to support himself.

The problem wasn't that John lacked a work ethic, it was that his strategy was faulty. The American Psychological Association (APA) put out a report that the inability to focus for even ten minutes on any one thing at a time may be costing you 20 to 40 percent in terms of efficiency and productivity. With so many things to focus on, it's difficult to be effective or efficient when doing the most important things. During the day, your body is sitting at a desk, but your mind may be somewhere else. You see, most of us are rarely present at work or in life. More often we're thinking of the next thing we need to do and then trying constantly to catch up.

The bottom line is that the conventional time-management approach to work is outdated and we're in need of a progressive attention management approach, or the ability to effectively focus on what is most important right now.

John and I looked at his past behavior, and he was able to acknowledge how his incessant multitasking was increasing his stress and making it more difficult to focus effectively at work.

We talked about his approaching tasks at work much as he would a meditation to train his mind. When he was e-mailing, he would allow that to be the object of attention for that moment, and when his mind wandered off to surfing the Web, talking to a coworker, or entertaining a mind trap, he would, without judgment, practice "See, touch, go" and gently return to the e-mail.

If he was in a business meeting, he would set the intention to listen, and when his eyes wandered onto his most recent text, tweet, or Facebook message, he would notice he was in a space of awareness and gently guide his attention back to listening. He could do the same with working on a project.

When he noticed a space where his mind was overwhelmed and cluttered, he would practice dropping into the body and saying to himself, "Breathing in, I calm my body, breathing out, I clear my mind."

As he practiced at work and continued to nonjudgmentally guide his mind back to what was most important in the now, he felt less stressed and saw the overwhelming pile of projects shrinking, and others around him commented on how focused he seemed. He began to feel more confident, energetic, and relaxed and happier at work. It was the Now Effect at work.

Choose a task at work today or this week, and treat it like a meditation.

○ E-MAIL MEDITATION. When you're e-mailing, e-mail for a certain period of time, and practice "See, touch, go" when your mind or behavior wanders.

○ PREPARING-FOR-A-MEETING MEDITATION. Benjamin Franklin said, "By failing to prepare, you are preparing to fail." There's truth in this; we feel better and more confident when we prepare. When you're preparing for a meeting, ask yourself how much time you really need. Whether it's fifteen, thirty, or sixty minutes, it is now your meditation time. As phone calls, texts, and messages come raining in, notice any impulses to get distracted, see if you can determine what that impulse feels like in the body, and then come back to the task at hand. Becoming curious about the physical impulse can prime your mind to notice it sooner, free you from being enslaved by it, and make you more effective.

○ BUSINESS MEETING MEDITATION. When you're in a business meeting and you notice your mind starting to get distracted and swim with all the other things you have to do that day, practice STOP, maybe noticing the tension in your body rising, and gently come back to your intention of being in the meeting, listening and engaging.

o WALKING-DOWN-THE-HALLWAY MEDITATION. This is a favorite of mine. As you walk around the office, pay attention to the movement of walking and the feeling of the floor beneath your feet. Or, as you walk, practice saying to yourself, "Breathing in, I am here at work, breathing out, I relax my body."

27

THINKING SMALL
CAN PRODUCE BIG RESULTS

More often than not, when I run into a person I haven't seen in a while and ask him or her, "Hey, how are you?" the response is overwhelmingly and eerily the same: "I'm doing okay, just really busy."

Busyness is a growing epidemic. Although we have lots of gadgets that are meant to make us more efficient with our time, they suck up all of our attention and life seems to speed up. What happens when life speeds up? You probably guessed it; we fall into autopilot. Whatever we were trying to do that was best for us falls to the bottom of the to-do list.

When I meet with clients I'll often say, "So you have this seemingly unending to-do list. Where is something for your own self-care on this list?" This question is often met with either a quizzical look or a moment of reflection, and then the answer is almost always "I'm not on it. There's no time for me."

When we dig a bit deeper, we often find some rigid underlying thoughts about what constitutes taking time for oneself. Check this out for yourself. Maybe you have a rule in your mind that in order to exercise you need an hour or more to go to a gym, or to practice playing guitar you need to set aside thirty minutes or more in a quiet place. Or maybe the only way to relax is to go on a vacation, or to be social you need to host an event or attend a gathering of some kind.

What if you engaged a beginner's mind and thought smaller? What if you were more flexible about what you could do with your time?

A group of my friends got together and created something called "75/50/20." That stood for 75 jumping jacks, 50 sit-ups, and 20 push-ups. Each day, on a group chat, we checked in when we had done the 75/50/20. I found myself doing them before dinner, in the office, at the beach, in someone's house, and at a park. It took all of five minutes to do and felt great.

Allow your mind to entertain the idea that you can do the things you like during the small moments of the day. You simply need to notice the spaces.

now moment

Take one thing that you've been meaning to do, and see if you can chip away at it in smaller moments during the day. For example, is there anywhere in your day when you have five minutes to do some push-ups or sit-ups? Are there twenty minutes at lunchtime to take a walk around your building or block?

For guitar or any skill that needs practice and reinforcement, there are many free videos online that offer five-minute instructions. Pick up your guitar and play for five to ten minutes; that is perfectly fine. Doing that a number of times will either give you the motivation to create more space in your day for guitar practice or simply improve your playing. It's really a win-win.

Maybe you will start with only five minutes a day; that is absolutely fine. Watch out for the subtle snap judgment that says you can't do it for this or that reason. You don't need to be ruled by mind traps. See the space between your awareness and the mind trap, view your life with fresh eyes, and move beyond the mind trap into action, no matter how small or brief.

part IV

PRIMING YOUR MIND FOR GOOD

Imagine that you are walking down the street and five people walk by you. Four of those people greet you with some form of salutation and a compliment such as "Hey, how you doing, you're looking good." Then one person walks by and says, "You're a jerk, and your hair looks terrible today." Which one sticks out in your mind? If you're like most people, the negative comment seems to be stickier. In fact, if I were to hook up your brain to a brain-imaging machine, we would see a greater surge of electrical activity in your brain connected to the negative comment. The fact is, the brain is more sensitive to unpleasant events than to pleasant ones.

Our brains are built this way to keep us out of danger. If we walk up a path and come to a fork in the road, one that has bear tracks on it and one that doesn't, our brains will automatically shift our attention to the bear tracks and send us a warning not to take that route.

The problem is that our brains exert this negativity in other areas of our life, and without an awareness of this negativity we have a greater likelihood of living with the glass half empty.

Take our relationships, for example. John Gottman, PhD, one of the leading researchers in the field of relationships, has developed a very keen system to conclude quickly whether a relationship will work or not. He carefully charted the number of times couples fought versus the number of times they interacted positively. He found that relationships that had an equal amount of negative versus positive interactions were likely to fail. In fact, the ratio for success was having at least five positive interactions to one negative interaction. That's because our brain makes a bigger deal out of negative events and interactions.

Without an awareness of this negativity bias, we can allow it to seep into the way we see life, which can have profound effects, creating everything from everyday stress to procrastination to anxiety and even depression. However, with awareness, we can begin to notice the spaces where we get hooked into this bias, step outside of them, and gain a wiser perspective.

To influence and balance out this subconscious negativity bias, we need to incline our minds toward the good in life. One simple way to do this is to pause once in a while and ask yourself, "What is good right now?" Don't look for an answer; just see what arises naturally.

Throughout this section you will be learning practical ways to train your mind to be kinder and more compassionate, hopeful, grateful, loving, giving, forgiving, and aware of the meaningful moments in life.

I'm not advocating that you wear rose-colored glasses; I'm simply saying that turning your mind toward the good will sow seeds of happiness and bolster your resilience during difficult times.

BE KIND WHENEVER POSSIBLE.
IT IS ALWAYS POSSIBLE.

No act of kindness, no matter how small, is ever wasted.

—AESOP

The Dalai Lama made a radical statement when he said, "Be kind whenever possible. It is always possible."

When someone cuts you off on the highway or another shopper has fourteen items in the ten-items-or-less express line at the supermarket, is kindness possible? How about when you're feeling particularly stressed, anxious, or depressed? Is kindness possible then? When someone is abusive toward you, can you be expected to respond with kindness?

What about kindness toward ourselves? Many find that this is the most difficult practice of all. Maybe we grew up in a house in which we weren't given attention, or perhaps we were abused and developed the belief that we aren't worthy of kindness. Or maybe a past trauma has created a steel case around our heart, making it difficult to accept kindness from ourselves or others.

Unfortunately, our minds rely on our memories to make decisions on how to relate to others today. In order to truly heal, we need to open our hearts. Creating a kind mind begins with ourselves.

The poet Hafiz writes in his poem "It Felt Love":

> How did the rose
> Ever open its heart
> And give to this world
> All its beauty?
> It felt the encouragement of light
> Against its being,
> Otherwise,
> We all remain
> Too frightened.

It's easier to open up and reveal our own gifts to the world when we feel positive, loving encouragement within. Our walls begin to come down when we feel safe, secure, and supported.

The truth is, kindness is often contagious, and if a few more of us were infected by it and spread it, we might soon have more nurturing environments at home, at work, and in public places.

Kindness is considered a virtue, something highly valued, in many traditions, including the field of psychology. It can be nurtured intentionally through little acts during the day.

Is kindness always possible? Perhaps not, but it can be an aspiration, or we can think of it as the light to guide our intention.

Make a commitment to be on the lookout for kindness. Are there spaces where your impulse is to act with indifference when you could instead recognize the choice point, break with routine, and act with kindness? Thinking about this now already inclines your mind to be aware of it. You might consider smiling at the checkout clerk, taking a bubble bath, listening to your partner, practicing meditation, or creating some space in which to breathe. There are so many ways to bring kindness into your life.

Perhaps you can think of some people who could use some kindness; maybe it's you. Picture them in your mind, and send them friendly wishes. You can hold them in your heart and say, "May you be safe and protected from inner and outer harm," "May you be happy," "May you be free from fear," "May you be healthy in body and mind."

Play with these phrases, create your own. Try this exercise in the spaces of your day, and see what happens. Bringing more kindness into your life in these ways can be a springboard to opening and nurturing your heart, which can lead to psychological healing and feelings of well-being.

29

COMPASSION IS A VERB

Goodness is the only investment that never fails.

—HENRY DAVID THOREAU

After losing her parents in the Holocaust, Hilde Back found refuge in Sweden as a preschool teacher. She knew what it felt like to live under adverse conditions and felt the tugging of her heart to help others who were disadvantaged. Every month Hilde put a few kronor (the Swedish currency) into an envelope and sent it off to a rural Kenyan student named Chris Mburu to help pay for his primary and secondary education. When she sponsored Chris Mburu, she did so as a gesture from her heart, with the hope that it would help in some small way. For Chris, Hilde's gesture was a gift of grace that allowed him to take advantage of a rare and privileged opportunity. Years later, he graduated from Harvard Law School and became a human rights lawyer for the United Nations. Hilde's small act of compassion opened his mind and heart and planted the seed for Chris to start the Hilde Back Education Fund, which offers rural Kenyan children a life of possibility.

Compassion is not some fuzzy feel-good concept. In the corporate, health care, scientific, and spiritual communities, strong efforts and equally impressive amounts of funding are targeted at bringing compassion into society's awareness on a large scale. For example, I designed a program for mindfulness in the workplace that eMindful and Kyra Bobinet, MD, MPH, Aetna's medical director for health and wellness innovation, have brought to Aetna's corporate and individual clients. Chade-Meng Tan at Google is the founding patron of Stanford University's Center for Compassion and Altruism Research and Education (CCARE). In 2008, Dr. Richard Davidson, the director of the Waisman Laboratory for Brain Imaging and Behavior, received a $2.5 million grant to study the neuroscience of compassion.

Compassion builds on empathy. Whereas empathy is a way of putting ourselves into another's shoes, compassion takes it a step further and is best described as the opening of the heart with a genuine desire to ease our own or someone else's suffering.

Compassion is not an automatic response. The typical initial reaction to the pain we hold or the pain of another is to turn away or disconnect. Imagine being around someone who is very anxious or depressed; it's far more likely that your mind will react with some kind of aversion. You'd rather not engage with that person; it's too uncomfortable.

To truly understand what compassion is, it's helpful to understand what compassion is not. Compassion is not about enabling or perpetuating a person's harmful behavior. This has been referred to as "idiot compassion." Offering drugs or alcohol to somebody who suffers from an addiction because you can't stand to see him or her in pain is not an act of compassion, because it enables further suffering.

Allowing someone who is struggling emotionally to be verbally or physically abusive to you is certainly not being compassionate toward either of you, because it perpetuates the other person's unhealthy state of mind.

Compassion isn't pity. The two are easily confused; pity doesn't have any association with feeling loving or caring, but compassion does. Pity is when you feel bad for someone but may feel no genuine desire to help him or her.

My friend and colleague Christopher Germer, PhD, a clinical instructor at Harvard Medical School who is well-known for his work with mindfulness and self-compassion, grew up with a great fear of public speaking. Over time he began to connect with the spaces of awareness in his life and systematically engage in compassion practices. He would intentionally practice and repeat connecting to his heart over and over again, "showering himself in love" and wishing himself to be well, free from fear, and at ease.

One day when he was speaking onstage, the fear came over him, physically gripping him, and in that moment, without his even being conscious of it, phrases of kindness and compassion began to wash over him. It's as if he had reprogrammed the subconscious snap judgment to be "It's going to be okay."

The speech was great. This is the Now Effect in action.

Everyone suffers from some form of stress and pain. There are many opportunities to practice compassion. Start looking around in public or at work and observe whether anyone seems to be struggling. Put yourself in his shoes and see if you feel any inclination to help, even by simply wishing him well.

As the acclaimed author, poet, and Vietnamese Buddhist monk Thich Nhat Hanh says, "Compassion is a verb," and your single action can have a ripple effect that spreads across many people's lives.

Compassion is not only a feeling, it is a skill that can be practiced, repeated, and cultivated in the spaces of our personal and professional lives. Think of yourself, someone else, or a group of people that is suffering right now. Sense the sorrow and pain they've experienced over time. You can't directly change them or fix their pain, but in this moment see if you can connect with your heart, opening to and noticing if there is an inclination to want to help in some way. Perhaps simply hold this person or group in your heart, wishing them wellness, safety from harm, and happiness. What you may be feeling is the heart of compassion, which is critical to healing ourselves and others. If any thoughts arise that call for action to help, consider what it might look like. Where are the spaces in your life in which you can do this? Remember, a small act can have big results.

30

I THINK I CAN, I THINK I CAN

In Watty Piper's classic story *The Little Engine That Could*, a long train had to be pulled over a very high mountain. When the large engines were asked to help, they looked at that high mountain in disbelief and said, "I can't; that is too much of a pull for me." Engine after engine continued to give excuses until the train asked the little switch engine, which puffed, "I think I can, I think I can." As it neared the top of the mountain, it started moving much slower but kept on, saying, "I think I can, I think I can, I think I can," as it eventually pulled the train over the peak.

For quite some time psychologists and business leaders have been looking into hope as an effective way of motivating people, dealing with difficult emotions, and cultivating well-being.

Hope isn't only a thought; it appears to be a synthesis of emotions and thoughts that allows us to believe we can reach certain goals. There's no question about it, hope is a strength. Hope motivates us, helps us break through difficult emotions, aligns our actions with our best interests, and cultivates a greater sense of ease from day to day.

Hope isn't a trait that some people have and others don't. It's a skill that we can cultivate. The late Rick Snyder, PhD, was an eminent psychologist who said that hope is fostered when we have a goal in mind, a determination that a goal can be reached, and a plan for how to reach that goal. In that sense, we can hope for big things (being elected president of the United States) or we can hope for small things (getting the dishes done tonight).

Sometimes we have a goal in mind, and when one plan fails to achieve that goal, we feel that the prospect of ever achieving it is hopeless. A key aspect of cultivating hope is flexibility and openness to change and having a backup plan (or two) in case the first doesn't work out. Like the little engine that could, when faced with a problem or a setback that gets in the way of achieving our goals, we can say to ourselves, "I think I can, I think I can," and power through to the top.

the hope scale

To gauge how you are doing in any particular moment, you can check in with what I call a hope scale. Here's how it works: Think about a time when you weren't feeling well and your prospects seemed dim. On a scale of 1 to 10, you might say your hope was a 2 or 3. Then consider the moments when things started to get better and your hope began to rise. What was the difference? When your hope was at the lower end of the scale, you were likely a bit depressed and could not envision a light at the end of the tunnel. You might have had a few ideas about how to get to that light, but your motivation and determination were hard to find. As your hope increased, you might have noticed a shift in your thoughts about what feeling better might be like, been able to envision more concrete options to experience greater pleasure, and felt an increase in your motivation to continue feeding your well-being.

It's important to say that I'm not advocating cultivating a sense of false hope or optimism that involves valiantly trying to make ourselves believe something that cannot be. No matter how high my hopes, I'm probably not going to be able to fly by flapping my arms. True hope takes an active path toward a potentially attainable goal, with a plan and the thought "I think I can."

Take a moment and consider how your life might benefit from some more hope. What would change if you had more hope about your life and your future?

now moment

Consider all the places in your life where your mind tells you what you can't do. Does it say that you'll never get promoted, never get married, never lose ten pounds? Does your mind tell you that you can't face a current obstacle?

What would your life be like in the days, weeks, and months ahead if you focused more on what you can do instead of what you can't do? Cultivating hope is like building a muscle; keep at it little by little, and it will get stronger.

Try to envision something realistic you want for yourself. Now create a plan for how to get there and, like the little engine that could, keep saying "I think I can."

31

GIVE UP ALL HOPE
FOR A BETTER PAST

Lily Tomlin once said, "Forgiveness means giving up all hope for a better past."

On hearing this quote most people react in one of two ways: either by saying "Aha!" or by laughing because it is so true. When we refuse to forgive, it's as if we're holding on to the past and saying, "See, past, I'm not going to let you have the pleasure of my letting go of you." Meanwhile, the past is the past; we can't change what happened, but we can change the meaning we give to it.

The truth is, the past is happening right now, in the present moment—if we let it. I'm not suggesting that we completely forget the past because the past is our teacher; however, I am suggesting that we loosen our grip on it.

There is a common misperception that forgiveness means condoning an act. Instead, it means releasing the bad thing that happened and breaking free from the torturous cycle that continues to reside within.

You have already been wronged once; why continue to let something in the past cause you pain by holding on to it? Many people maintain the erroneous belief that holding on to past events somehow hurts the other person. It does not. It hurts only yourself. In fact, the practice of forgiveness has been shown to reduce stress, anger, and depression and support many aspects of well-being and happiness.

Thich Nhat Hanh says, "When there is a mature relationship between people, there is always compassion and forgiveness."

Through compassion and forgiveness those who are suffering can come to terms with the way things are and slowly let go of past atrocities that, through dwelling on them, remain in the spaces of their present lives.

We can begin to forgive, even though we will never forget.

It's important to know that forgiveness is not a process that occurs instantly. You may need time to reach a place of forgiveness. If the act is fresh, you may need some distance from it before engaging in this work. Even when the time is right, it will likely take practice, as the tides of anger and hatred will bring you back to holding the grudge.

now moment

Allow this to be a choice point to practice forgiveness. Think of someone who has hurt you or caused you pain (maybe not the person who has hurt you most) whom you are holding a grudge against right now. Visualize the time you were hurt by this person and feel the pain you still carry. Hold tightly to your unwillingness to forgive. Now observe what emotion you are feeling. Is it anger, resentment, sadness? Also use your body as a barometer and notice physically

www.youtube.com/NowEffect

what you feel. Are you tense anywhere or feeling heavy? Now bring awareness to your thoughts: Are they hateful, spiteful thoughts?

Feel this burden that lives inside when you hold so tightly to past hurts. Now ask yourself, "Who is suffering? Have I carried this burden long enough? Am I willing to forgive?" If not, that is okay; perhaps the time will come when you're ready.

If you are ready, practice "Breathing in, I acknowledge the pain, breathing out, forgiving and releasing this burden from my heart and mind."

Continue this as long as it is supportive to you.

COUNT YOUR BLESSINGS

Imagine that I am a professor and you are a student in my class. One day I split the class into three groups: I ask the first group to spend the week writing down five things they are grateful for each day, the second group to write down five things that burden them, and the third group to write down five neutral events. If you are in the first group, over the course of the week you will likely find yourself feeling better, perhaps even happier, than those in the other two groups.

The thirteenth-century theologian and philosopher Meister Eckhart said, "If the only prayer you said in your whole life was 'Thank you,' that would suffice."

However, believe it or not, often beneath our awareness, our minds are very busy counting our perceived burdens. It could be happening right now. Counting our burdens depletes our energy, and our minds can spiral down into feeling stressed, anxious, or depressed.

Our subconscious minds are not primed to frame gratitude in a positive light. For many of us, gratitude has been experienced in the past as something that is rote and devoid of real meaning. Maybe we were forced to be grateful around the table while growing up and resented it, or maybe a therapist told us that being grateful would alleviate our depression and it didn't. Or maybe we're so attached to being angry that we don't want to feel grateful. If we try to count our blessings, our mind may jump in with some form of automatic judgment such as "That's ridiculous, I don't see how that can help" or "Been there, done that."

The result of being ruled by those automatic thoughts is that they keep you from intentionally engaging with fresh eyes. There may be a reason for it. Perhaps it's too painful to open your heart, or maybe you believe that if you try you'll be disappointed or, worse, you'll get hurt. If this resistance arises, you can bring a beginner's mind to it, notice where the resistance lies in your body, and, with kind attention, accept the reality of it, not judging it as good or bad. Be open and welcoming to what's there; perhaps it has something to teach you. After you investigate it, redirect your attention to counting your blessings.

now moment

Pause, close your eyes, and drop this question into your mind: "What am I grateful for right now?" Don't look for anything in particular; just see what arises.

After you open your eyes, here are five things to consider:

1. Are you in good health? Do you have a roof over your head? Do you have a good job?
2. Are there people in your life whom you appreciate?
3. If you have children, are they healthy?
4. Has anyone smiled at you today?

5. Do you have freedom of speech, the right to vote, and the freedom to practice the religion of your choice?

The fact that you're alive means that there's more right with you than wrong and you can be grateful for what's right. I promise, there's no better time than now to start weaving a web of gratitude.

Don't stop there; make a conscious effort to drop the question into your mind to see what you are grateful for at the end of each day for at least a week. Write the answers down, and notice how it feels to count your blessings.

33

PRESENT NOSTALGIA

See the positive side, the potential, and make an effort.
—THE DALAI LAMA

In the musical *Rent* the cast sings that there are 525,600 minutes in a year and that some people measure them in sunsets, cups of coffee, laughter, or tears of joy. The song and musical bring awareness to the moments of our lives and how very precious they truly are.

The problem is, it's all too common not to know what we have until it's gone. This shift to living on automatic blinds us to what is sacred in the moment. Having to struggle financially as a student, for example, was a source of stress at the time but later is remembered as an exciting, creative time. Sitting with kids when they're sick doesn't seem much fun to a parent, but later, when the kids have grown up, it's looked back upon as a sweet time together.

The very things that in the moment dampen our mood can later be sources of intense gratification, nostalgia, and delight.

Is there a way to reconnect with the sacred moments of daily life? Is there a way we can become more aware that hidden in the moments that seem burdensome there may be something precious? Present nostalgia is the ability to bring that warm feeling, longing, and meaning, which usually arrive after the experience is gone, into the moment.

Thinking about the present as if it were the past is a way of tricking your mind into being more open to your inner wisdom and allowing you to see more clearly what really matters. Why wait until the moment passes to reap its benefits?

now moment

Create present nostalgia. Imagine yourself many years from now looking back onto your younger self in this moment. What is it about this time that is precious? What's here that may not be here later on? What advice might that older and perhaps wiser self have for you? Is there something in your life that is precious that you could intentionally pay more attention to? Perhaps you're stressed about work, and your older, wiser self might tell you to practice letting go of work and spend more time with your family. Or maybe you take your body for granted, thinking it's indestructible, and your wiser self would highlight the importance of eating better or including some light stretching in your activities. Maybe you just had a child and don't yet realize how quickly they grow up.

Practice being on the lookout for these precious moments throughout the day.

34

A SMILE IS A SOURCE OF JOY

Thich Nhat Hanh reminds us that "Sometimes your joy is the source of your smile, but sometimes your smile can be the source of your joy." Try this little experiment. Get a pen and put it between your teeth horizontally. Now breathe in and out; notice the sensations of muscles in your face, and be aware of how you feel emotionally. When thoughts of "This is silly" or "Why am I doing this?" arise, just notice them as thoughts and come back to paying attention to how you are feeling.

What did you find?

Marsha Linehan, PhD, calls this the "Half-Smile Experiment." She found that when people tried this, they found that their mood changed. Marsha is the creator of Dialectical Behavior Therapy (DBT), a skills-training approach to helping with distress tolerance and emotional balance.

Think about it: we feel different when we walk around with our head held high than when we slump over looking at the ground, just as we feel different when we smile than when we frown.

Try slumping over, looking at your lap, and saying, "I am amazing!" Or try sitting up straight, looking forward, and saying, "I am a failure." Neither of those feels quite right because the body language doesn't match the thought. Many therapies advocate working through our bodies and behaviors as a way of bringing joy and happiness into our lives.

There are other subtle ways to work with our mood through our bodies. Consider when you're with a friend. Are you slouching, representing a mood of being closed down and tired, or are you standing up straight, bringing a sense of openness and alertness to your interaction?

If we drop into a space of awareness, we can notice what our body is saying and then choose to shift it to the position it would be in if we were feeling good.

now moment

To bring more smiling and joy into our lives, we can try integrating the following short poetic verse by Thich Nhat Hanh with our breathing.

No matter where you are, practice saying to yourself: "Breathing in, I calm my body, breathing out, I smile."

You can shorten it so that when you breathe in you say "Calm" and when you breathe out you say "Smile." If you don't feel like physically smiling, you can cast a kind, gentle smile inwardly at yourself or at some physical or emotional pain you are experiencing. This will still activate areas of the brain that would light up if you were physically smiling.

35

DO SMALL THINGS WITH GREAT LOVE

Mother Teresa said, "We can do no great things—only small things with great love."

Though this quote can be seen as embodying the essence of humility, there's also a different way to see it.

What if you were able to draw on this message when you are feeling overwhelmed as a reminder that you don't have to do any great thing in that moment (for example, cleaning the entire house, working out for an hour, making a gourmet dinner) but instead can do smaller things with great love? This not only breaks down the barrier against moving forward but also waters the seeds of self-kindness and self-love.

I was explaining this concept to a man I was working with who was an artist. He made pottery. He said, "I don't understand; when I make a pot, I just go ahead and make it. However, I'm not feeling motivated to make pottery lately, so I just don't do it. I'm such a failure." As we spoke about his making pots, we began to break down his work into smaller tasks.

He had to decide which clay to buy, get his tools prepared, wedge the clay, and then shape it, among other steps.

I asked him, "What if this didn't have to be one great act but small acts with great love?" We talked about being more present with the small steps and not putting so much pressure on achieving the finished project.

As he returned to work, of course his mind often wandered onto the finished product, and at times he became overwhelmed. When he noticed that he was stuck, he recognized that he was in a space of awareness and brought a beginner's mind to the moment, not judging it, coming back to his breath, and bringing his intention and attention back to working with the "small thing" with "great love." He kept it simple: when he was buying the clay, he was buying the clay; when he was getting his tools, he was getting his tools; when he was shaping the clay, he was shaping the clay. He got back into touch with the feel of the clay, the satisfaction of seeing the picture in his mind take shape, and the pleasure of using his favorite tools, all of which helped him relax into the moment. At times he noticed his mind jumping to the pleasure others were going to derive from a pot, and that made him feel good.

When our minds start to feel overwhelmed by the mountains of work before us, we can always bring ourselves back to the present by anchoring our attention to our breath or body and choosing to recalibrate, bringing our awareness to the small tasks we can do in the moment.

Sometimes in the morning my mind begins to swim with all the work I have to do that day. However, I can't jump into work immediately, as it's often my job to make breakfast for my family. When thinking about the mountain of work I have, initially I often get frustrated while preparing the food. When I notice this, I know it's a choice point, and I come back to focusing on doing one thing at a time and remembering that I am nourishing myself and my family so we can be well in this world and pass that wellness on to others. Sometimes I imbue the moment with love by repeating in my mind, "May this food support us all in being healthy in body and mind." Though this isn't a panacea, it's a simple gesture that often changes my experience of making breakfast and, ultimately, how I start my day.

now moment

Choose something that you want to accomplish that can ignite feeling overwhelmed. Maybe it's a growing pile of dishes in the sink that you can tackle one dish at a time or perhaps files need to be organized that you can do one by one, or maybe there's an onslaught of e-mails that you can answer five minutes at a time. Experiment with breaking tasks down and bringing great love to small things. Think about how what you're doing is benefiting others. Even with e-mail you can think, "May my work here be a source of support to my family and colleagues." We can turn the small stuff into opportunities to prime our minds for good and practice cultivating the Now Effect.

THE SEEDS OF RESILIENCY

Richard Shankman is a mindfulness teacher who spent years taking mindfulness programs to state prisons and drug and alcohol rehab centers. It didn't take long for him to respond when the opportunity arose to take a five-week program to inner-city children at Emerson Elementary in Oakland, California. They were kids who struggled with adversity and didn't seem to have much peace or promise in their lives. When ABC News caught wind of the program, it went over to check out what was going on and interviewed Richard and the students.

One fourth grader in the program said, "Before a test, if I'm nervous, I just breathe, calm down, and it sends a message to my mind that I can make it!"

Even in the face of adversity, the positive feelings of calm and hope naturally arose. This is the Now Effect in action. The practices they had been doing influenced that young boy's belief system and this could very well change the rest of his life. Richard went on to cofound Mindful Schools, which has touched the lives of more than ten thousand children and more than a thousand adults.

Researchers have been looking into what sows the seeds of resiliency. Resiliency gives us the ability to roll with the punches or, when we're knocked down, to get up more quickly.

In Dr. Richard Davidson's study on the brain and resiliency there were two groups; one went through an eight-week Mindfulness-Based Stress Reduction (MBSR) program and the other did not. The subjects who did the MBSR program showed more significant increases in activity in the left side of the brain, which is associated with positive emotions and regulation of emotions, than the control group did. The MBSR group also showed an increase in antibodies to a flu vaccine, providing neuroscientific proof of the benefits of mindfulness and resiliency.

George, a forty-two-year-old man suffering from obsessive-compulsive disorder and panic attacks, came to a mindfulness group I was leading. One day during the group meeting I noticed that he was beginning to breathe faster and sweat was forming on his brow. I asked him how he was doing, and he told the group that he thought he was having a panic attack. We all paused as I led him through the STOP practice. After it was over, his breath appeared steadier and he seemed calmer. His eyes opened, brimming with tears, and he said, "I can do this," as he moved out of the moment of difficulty and into a place of greater balance.

As we learn how to drop down out of the maelstroms of our minds and into the here and now, we cultivate a sense of self-trust and self-reliance that breeds a strength that allows for a quicker return to balance. Throughout this section, reading about priming your mind for good and certainly engaging in the practices have already been encouraging a resilient mind.

part V

KNOW YOUR BRAIN, CHANGE YOUR MIND

Stacey was a client of mine who lost her father to a heart attack when she was three years old. She spent a lot of time being angry at her dad for not taking care of himself and leaving her in this world without him. Through time and therapy she reached a place of forgiveness, and the anger didn't grip her as tightly anymore. Whenever there was the slightest indication, however, that someone she cared about was retreating from her life, she experienced a surge of fear, tears flooded her eyes, and her emotions overwhelmed her. In my office she would often ask, "What's wrong with me? I know this person's not really going to leave, so why do I always get so overwhelmed?"

One day when she experienced this overwhelming feeling, I had her practice a mindful check-in. As she came down from the drama in her mind and her emotions calmed a bit, we started talking about the impact of emotional trauma on the brain. The experience of her father passing when she was young had been so scary that it had likely wired her nervous system to react strongly to any perception of being left, in the same way as when a dog bites you, you can later become instantly scared in the presence of other dogs.

I told her, "It's not actually you who is creating this reaction; your brain immediately downshifts to the 'fear circuit' before you're even aware of it. It's not your fault; there's nothing wrong with you. The neural highways in our brains get wired together through the experiences we have over time, and we can retrain your brain so that it doesn't automatically react in this fashion."

I asked her to envision a neural network in her brain that held her pain, judgments, shame, and fear about her dad's death. Whenever there was a threat of someone leaving, her network became activated, igniting all those feelings once again.

In that moment, she was present and able to see the space between her awareness and her brain's reactivity. In that space she understood that she was much more than her brain's reactions. From there we started working toward Stacey relating to herself in a new way and changing the rest of her life.

The message in this section is simple: getting to know the brain provides another opportunity to step outside the chaos in the mind and relate *to* your experiences instead of *from* your experiences. This moves you into the now, into a choice point where you have the chance to respond differently. As you move through this section, you'll get to know your brain. You'll be able to picture what's happening in there when your buttons are pushed or your brain is on autopilot, and you will learn what areas you need to activate to come back into balance and ignite the growth of a healthier and more compassionate mind.

Little by little, as we widen our perspective and find the space of clarity where new possibilities can unfold, we continue to water the seeds of the Now Effect.

HI, I'M YOUR BRAIN

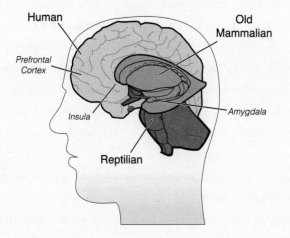

The brain is a complex, mysterious, and awe-inspiring organ that even the most brilliant neuroscientists have very little clue about. What we do know is that there are really three brains inside our heads (many scientists call this the "triune theory of the brain"). Getting acquainted with the basic functions of the brain will help you visualize it and create a space between your awareness and the experiences you're having, leading to more choice points.

The most primitive part of your brain is called the brain stem; it's your "first brain." It's been called the "reptilian brain" because it acts in the same way as a lizard's brain. It's the fastest and most impulsive part of the brain and gets us ready for action, sparking the fight, flee, or freeze response. You don't want to have to stop and deliberate about what to do when a car is coming at you; you react automatically. Its neurons also regulate basic functions, such as breathing and circulation, and our states of arousal (waking, sleeping, and so on). Most important, it's always active whether we're awake or asleep.

The limbic region is the "second brain" and is considered a primitive part of the brain, hence the nickname "old mammalian brain." It's been called the "animal brain" because your cat or dog has the same kind of brain. This area is also the emotional center of the brain. It makes our emotionally influenced snap judgments. The limbic region also holds the memory of facts and our personal experiences. It also makes it possible for us to feel connected and attached to other people and animals. An integral part of the limbic system is the amygdala, which is known as the "fear circuit." The amygdala, which is tightly linked with the hippocampus, accesses memories of past experiences that include fear, rage, and at times even pleasure, leading us to react with survival instincts.

Wrapped around all of this is the "third brain," the cortex. *Cortex* is Latin for "bark," because that's what it looks like, and it's similar to an outer shell. It wasn't until soldiers started coming back from the Great War (aka World War I) with brain injuries that scientists discovered that this brain has special sections dedicated to speech, vision, and memory. Many neuroscientists believe that the cortex has the most plasticity, which means it is the part we have the greatest ability to change.

Right behind your forehead is the prefrontal cortex or, as some people call it, the "human brain." This is the most evolved part of the brain and also the slowest to respond because it works through deliberate reflection and response, as opposed to immediate reaction. This area is what really sets us apart from other species. The prefrontal cortex is the area of the brain that hosts our capacity for decision making, planning, perceiving, reflecting, and orchestrating thoughts and actions.

There's another part of the brain that some scientists consider part of the prefrontal cortex and is the central switchboard responsible for linking communication between all the brains. This is a little nugget called the insula. It monitors the body to tell us if there's an itch, we're physically out of balance, or a situation is unfair. You might think of this as the seat of awareness. In fact, there is a direct connection between mindfulness practice and the growth of the insula.

These three brains together host about 100 billion brain cells or neurons. The number of connections between neurons has been estimated at 10,000,000,000,000,000. That is more connections than there are stars in our galaxy. So there's a lot going on under the hood. As you read this sentence, the billions of neurons, in your brain are sending electrical and chemical signals from one to the other to make sense of these words. Trying to really envision this can blow your mind. So let's move on.

At various times, one brain can be more active than another. If the cortex controls too much, we can be left living a very practical life that is empty of emotion. If we spend a lot of time downshifting from the cortex to the limbic region or brain stem, we can be overly impulsive and our passions and fears can dominate our lives.

What we're aiming for is a more integrated brain in which each area communicates with the others to help us stay connected to what really matters. This sets the stage for the following chapters.

38

DRIVING YOUR BRAIN (CRAZY)

f you were to ask my family about what I was like when I was younger, they would tell you without hesitation that it took only a little spark to set me off. I had a lot of anger and no idea how to manage it. As I grew older, I realized that getting angry all the time wasn't working for me. I began to put great effort into living a more balanced life, and what I discovered is exactly what you're reading in this book. We can all relate to acting impulsively when our buttons are pushed. Maybe we walk out to the car and find a flat tire, our kids spill their shakes on the floor, or our coworker makes yet another mistake. At that moment, the activity in our brain downshifts into the second or even first brain as our emotions start to take over, causing us to react instead of respond.

You can think of your brain as a vehicle and each of the three layers as gears that are shifted up and down throughout the day, often with an automatic transmission. We can be slowly deliberating in one moment, making conscious decisions, and in another moment getting our buttons pushed, instantly downshifting to lower regions of the brain that ignite feelings of anger, anxiousness, panic, and fear or accessing the fight, flee, or freeze response.

One benefit of downshifting into the "second brain," or limbic region, is to access our emotions, creating a sense of empathy and connecting to what another person is feeling. One benefit of downshifting to the brain stem is to get us out of danger quickly.

One consequence of the automatic downshifting is that we can become emotionally dysregulated, reacting to events with fear or anger, as I did as a kid. When our buttons are pushed and our brain downshifts, our autonomic nervous system is activated. That's the part of the brain that controls vital functions such as our breathing, heartbeat, and the functions of many other organs and glands. It is made up of two neural pathways, the sympathetic nervous system and the parasympathetic nervous system. You can think of the sympathetic nervous system as the accelerator and the parasympathetic nervous system as the brake.

When our buttons are pushed, the sympathetic accelerator kicks into gear, getting ready for the fight-or-flight response; we start breathing faster, our heart rate goes up, and we often lose sight of our rational mind. That's great if we're trying to avoid getting run over by a car; however, it's not so great when we can become impulsive, irritable, and prone to behavior we later regret at work and home.

When the brain downshifts in this way and we recognize it, we have entered into a space of awareness, another choice point where we can upshift and spread the brain activity to the prefrontal cortex. Now that we have access to some rational thought, we can choose to activate the brake, the parasympathetic nervous system. To come back into balance, I teach the people I work with how to maximize the amount of oxygen entering their bodies with deep belly breathing, a natural way of breathing.

Understanding when your brain has downshifted can help you recalibrate your emotional imbalance and get back to feeling centered.

now moment

There are many opportunities for our brains to downshift into more stressed, emotionally turbulent, or imbalanced states of mind. It may happen when we're about to go into a big business meeting, go on a first date, or stand up in front of an audience to speak. What we need in such moments is to upshift. If you've ever watched a puppy or a baby breathe, you've noticed that they breathe primarily into their bellies. For some reason, as adults, many of us breathe into our chests, as if we're on alert, keeping us in a state of downshift.

Whether your brain is in a state of upshift or downshift or just humming on neutral, take a moment to try this out.

- Lie down, place your hands on your belly, and just breathe. You may notice that you naturally breathe down into your belly and your hands rise and fall. If this is not the case, concentrate on bringing oxygen down to your abdomen until you notice your hands rising and falling with each breath.
- With each breath, count up to ten and back down to one.
- Try this out during the day in the spaces of your life, and do it when your buttons get pushed.

39

THE WONDERFUL WORLD OF GABA

Tom was a striking figure; at about six feet two inches with a sculpted hairstyle, he looked as though he had just walked out of a photo shoot. When we sat down in my office, he was clearly nervous. He told me he had never seen a therapist before. He was fidgeting, his voice was shaky, and his breathing was a bit fast and uneven.

Elisha: Can you tell me what you're feeling?

Tom: I'm feeling a bit nervous.

Elisha: I want to try something with you right now. Are you open to it?

Tom: Sure.

Elisha: Close your eyes for a moment; feel the connections of your feet to the floor and your body against the couch. Do you notice where you feel the fear in your body?

Tom: My chest is kind of tight.

Elisha: Okay, now, as you notice that feeling, say to your-
          self, "Fear, fear, fear."

In less than a minute Tom let out a deep exhalation.

Elisha: What just happened?
Tom: I don't know; the tension seems to have just dis-
          sipated.

If Tom and I had been able to peek inside his brain, we might have
seen the lower regions, such as the amygdala, or "fear circuit," firing up
when he was nervous. Then, when he expressed what he was feeling,
he activated the prefrontal cortex to send out a neurotransmitter
called gamma-aminobutyric acid (GABA) to wash over this fear
circuit and calm it down. GABA is our "natural Valium." It turns
down the volume of our fear and brings us into balance.

When we're disconnected from the now and lost in worries
about the future or resentments about the past, we don't have access to this wonderful natural chemical in our brains. However,
as soon as we step into the spaces of our lives, we can connect to
the prefrontal cortex and choose to summon it, to experience a
feeling of ease.

now moment

Picture a time when you were experiencing fear. As if you were
watching a movie, picture a "fear circuit" in the limbic region;
that is the amygdala flaring up. See the front of your brain sending "natural Valium" to wash over the amygdala and quench the
flames. Using your imagination this way can help depersonalize the

experience by helping you understand that you are not your fear. It is a circuit in your brain that you can choose to cool down. As you practice and repeat this exercise, you can train your mind to put a space between you and your fearful experience, giving you freedom from the stress response and allowing you to gain perspective on what truly matters.

THE NARRATOR

Josh was sitting outside a coffee shop sipping his tea when he noticed a couple next to him engaging in PDA (public display of affection). Immediately his mind perked up: *What's wrong with them? This is ridiculous.* It was impossible not to notice them, and as he did, he thought, *What's wrong with me? How come I'm not in a relationship?* Memories of his ex-girlfriend popped into his mind, and sadness about their recent breakup arose. He remembered all the good times. *Maybe I should go on one of those dating sites,* he thought, *but I'll never find a match.* He sank into his seat feeling more alone than ever.

When we engage with the stories in our minds at the expense of connecting with the direct experience of the present moment, we can get stuck in cycles of anxiety or depression.

The fact is, we are wired to tell stories. There's a cluster of regions in the brain that we can call the "narrative network." It goes straight up the center of the head and constantly tells stories about what we're doing, how we're doing, why something is good or bad or right or wrong, or how a problem can be fixed, or it wanders off into a daydream. We'll call this part of the brain the Narrator.

The Narrator lights up when we're in "default mode" or on autopilot. As Josh was sipping his tea, the Narrator took in the scenes, ran them through a filter, and created a story. Unfortunately, the story in Josh's mind ended with his being alone. We're trying to balance the Narrator with another key part of the brain known as the "experiential network," which we can call the Sensor. This area lights up when we're paying attention to our senses. Research shows that the two networks are inversely correlated, meaning that when one is very active, the other is less so. So when you're sipping tea or coffee and intentionally taking in the taste, as your senses come alive the Narrator is not as active. If your brain is on default mode or daydreaming while you're sipping, you're likely to miss out on tasting the drink.

We often perceive uncomfortable feelings as threats. The Narrator is then triggered beneath our awareness and begins to weave a story to counteract the perceived threat. But in the process it starts a cycle of rumination that unfortunately tends to dig us deeper into a feeling that something is wrong.

Identifying when the Narrator is at play creates a space between our awareness and the stories and judgments of our minds. In that space we can choose to activate the Sensor and feel the sensory experience of the here and now. We can also choose to stop interpreting the uncomfortable feeling as a threat and, rather than trying to escape from it, provide a more empathetic container, feeling what's there and giving it space.

now moment

Next time you're sipping a warm drink or eating food, take a moment to notice which network is more active. If it's the Narrator, try to intentionally shift to the Sensor. Or when you're feeling a strong emotion, recognize that it's likely activating the Narrator and what you need to do is activate the Sensor, which is connected to the now. You can practice a mindful check-in or say to yourself, "Breathing in, I calm my brain, breathing out, I feel my body."

_____

FREE YOUR MIND

Recently I was at the local playground, watching my son jumping off a step that was about six inches high. Each time he would get up on the step with glee, take a few moments to adjust his feet, and then jump with a huge smile and break out in laughter, clearly having the time of his life. It was amazing how much fun he could squeeze out of such a simple action. It made me wonder why adults lose sight of the joy in small things.

As it turns out, our brains are wired to "enslave" our present experiences with our past experiences so that we miss out on the uniqueness of what's happening in the now.

When a child comes across a flower, it's as if she's never seen a flower before, and she excitedly grabs it to show to an adult. When the adult sees the flower, his or her brain compares it to the thousands of flowers it has seen before and decides that this particular flower is not much different, not very important, and not worth the attention, so that before we even consciously see it, the decision is made to disregard it.

When the brain uses previous judgments, memories, and experiences to see the flower, it's called top-down processing. When the brain sees a flower as if for the first time, free from preconceived notions, it's called bottom-up processing.

Top-down processing isn't all bad—it's the source of our gut reactions, which keep us out of dark alleys and give us our ability to think on our feet. It allows past experience, memories, judgments, and beliefs to help us reach a conclusion about what needs to happen next.

Unfortunately, when our brains hold judgments such as "I can never be alone," "I have to do everything myself," or "Life is never going to turn out well for me," the judgments get in the way of experiencing the present. When someone smiles at you in the checkout line and you hold on to a belief that no one cares about you, the intent of a warm gesture will be missed.

If we can consciously shift our brains to bottom-up processing, we can see the world from a new perspective—as if through the eyes of a child.

now moment

To free my mind, when I smell a flower, I make it a practice to smell it twice. I let the first inhalation come and go, as I know that top-down processing is occurring and I'm not really getting at the essence of the flower. The second time I inhale the scent, my preconceptions have been cleared out and I can get a better sense of the uniqueness of the flower, as if it were the first flower I had ever smelled. By engaging in bottom-up processing, we can turn walking around the block into a playful practice. The next time you do this, be curious about one thing you encounter. It could be the smell of a flower, the sound of

birdsong, the sight of clouds, the touch of a breeze, or simply awareness of your physical sensations, emotions, or thoughts. As soon as
you notice your mind wandering off, you are in a space of awareness;
gently bring your attention back to your intention. Come back to
bottom-up processing and tune in to the direct experience of the
present moment.

42

"THAT'S NOT FAIR" NEURONS

Let's say I just found a twenty-dollar bill and offered to split it with you, but I would split it the way I wanted to. If you accept my offer, we both walk away with something; if you reject it, neither of us gets anything. My offer to you is $3. What do you say?

If you're like 75 percent of people, you'll reject it because your brain says, "No way, that's not fair." For some reason your brain doesn't register that at the end of the day you will receive either $3 or $0.

If I were to hook your brain up to a functional magnetic resonance imaging (fMRI) machine, we'd see that you'd likely have high activation in an area of the brain called the anterior insula, which often measures disgust, mistrust, or unfairness.

Let's call the neurons in this area the "that's not fair" neurons.

Research shows that more than half the people who make it a practice to connect with the present moment, for example, regular meditators, took the offer and showed no significant activity in these neurons.

What gives?

As you practice connecting with the now, you become more aware of emotions as they arise and are no longer swept up by them. You strengthen the brain's ability to measure internal body states (interoception). The better you are at consciously noticing a rapid heartbeat, flushed face, or tension in your shoulders, the more likely you are to take corrective action to calm your body down. The better you are at recognizing the urge to grab that next cigarette or piece of chocolate cake, the more likely you are to be aware of your ability to drop into the space of awareness and ride the urge with mindfulness. The thought "Hey, this isn't fair" is a judgment based on the emotion of disgust or perhaps anger that brings a host of physical sensations. An integrated brain sees the emotion and acknowledges it but is able to still engage the prefrontal cortex and open up the playing field to better choices and better decision making.

now moment

Is there an event that you are still holding on to as not fair? Maybe it's a recent speeding ticket, the last installment of taxes you had to pay, the division of chores in your house, or the extra pile of work you were given at the office. When you envision it, the "that's not fair" neurons fire up. The next time you notice this happening, see if you can get in touch with the feeling in your body, activate your brain, and picture the thought "That's not fair" as being simply an impersonal firing of a neuron in your brain. Ask yourself, "What's really most important right now?" to harness the ability to choose a healthier response.

43

YOUR INTUITIVE BRAIN

The neurologist Antonio Damasio and his colleagues studied patients with damage to the prefrontal cortex, the area of the brain that lies behind the forehead. They put four decks of cards in front of the patients. Two decks held cards that were high risk, paying $100 for winning cards and $350 for losing cards. The other two decks were more conservative, paying $50 for winning cards and $250 for losing cards. Patients were not told which decks had more risk, nor were they told that they had only a hundred cards to choose from.

By the fortieth or fiftieth card, most people develop a sense of which is the bad deck and which is the good deck, but the subjects with prefrontal damage continued to choose cards from the bad deck. They might have cognitively known that it wasn't the best deck, but it didn't feel wrong to them. That is similar to how they would act in everyday life, continuing to take big risks and missing the messages that this is the wrong path to follow.

Though a majority of us don't have damage to our prefrontal lobes, we sometimes act as though we do by falling into the same traps over and again. We know it isn't healthy for us to eat a tub of ice cream, but we do it anyway. We know that fighting with our spouse or friend isn't going to get the desired result, but we fall into that trap. We know that surfing the Web at work is going to lead to projects not getting done, but we continue to do so.

Damasio also hooked up participants to skin conductance response (SCR) machines that measured sweat on the skin, which is an anticipatory emotional signal from the body representing a gut feeling that something is wrong. Those with intact brains were sweating slightly on their palms after about ten cards of the bad deck, whereas those with the brain damage didn't sweat. This leads us to believe that the prefrontal cortex is responsible for getting messages from our bodies and developing reliable intuition.

Reliable intuition leads to reliable snap judgments. When we're able to connect with the sensory world of the body, we may be able to sense when something or someone is safe or dangerous. In the experiment with the cards, the brain's ability to perceive the sweat clued people in to the fact that they were engaging in risky behavior before they figured it out cognitively.

As we mindfully connect to our bodies, we strengthen the prefrontal cortex and our ability to pick up on physical signals sooner. As we practice tuning in to the now, we begin to find more spaces to respond from a place of insight and composure.

WIRED FOR EMPATHY
AND COMPASSION

If you want others to be happy, practice compassion. If you want to be happy, practice compassion.

—THE DALAI LAMA

In the early 1990s, in a small laboratory in Parma, Italy, a neurophysiologist, Giacomo Rizzolatti, was working with a group of colleagues using macaque monkeys to study the neurons that specialize in controlling hand and mouth movements. They hooked up macaque monkeys to monitors and gave them nuts to open. As one monkey was doing so, a scientist accidentally walked into the laboratory, picked up some nuts, and began to eat them. The monkey looked over at the scientist who was eating the nut, and although the monkey was not moving or actually eating the nut, its brain responded as if it were. Rizzolatti and his team couldn't understand what they were seeing, but as they repeated the action over and over, they came to understand that monkeys are wired with what are now called mirror neurons. Studying the monkeys led to studying humans, which showed that the motor area of the brain lights up when a person watches someone engaged in physical action. It also showed that the mirror neurons are activated when a person perceives someone else experiencing a feeling.

Mirror neurons map the intentions and feelings of another person to create a neural bridge of empathy. The neuroscientist V. S. Ramachandran calls them "empathy neurons" or "Dalai Lama neurons." People who rate high on a scale of empathy also show higher mirror neuron activity.

The discovery of mirror neurons has great implications for social intelligence. You can use your mirror neuron system to better understand and create empathy with your friends, family, colleagues, and clients. It can also help you understand how your experiences can be influenced by those around you.

Though research in this area is still in its infancy, it seems that we can develop or work out these areas of our brains by imagining connecting with others. Athletes have been exploiting their mirror neurons for years through using mental practice and imagery to improve their jump shots, hits, or kicks. In the same way, we can improve our empathy by firing our mirror neurons through imagining empathic situations or simply by being empathic with ourselves.

now moment

To develop empathy for yourself, the next time you feel sad, angry, or happy, take a moment to fully experience what you are feeling, mentally, physically, and emotionally. Then think about what you would do if a friend were experiencing the same emotion and extend the empathy you would feel for another to yourself.

To nurture your empathy for another, think back to a time when someone you know was experiencing an emotion such as joy, sadness, anger, or calm. Maybe it was during a situation at home or at work. Picture the scene in your mind, and see if you can feel what that person was feeling. Where do you feel it in your body? Fully experiencing what that person was feeling is possible because your mirror neurons are at play. A more empathic brain allows you to become aware of and connect to an emotion as it arises within you (or someone else) and, rather than reacting to the emotion, experience it in the now.

part VI

WORKING WITH DIFFICULT EMOTIONS

The thirteenth-century Sufi poet Rumi wrote, "This being human is a guest-house. Every morning a new arrival, a joy, a depression, a meanness. . . . Welcome and entertain them all!" You may think, "Welcome and entertain them all? Are you crazy? Why would I want to welcome and entertain those horribly uncomfortable feelings? All I want to do is get away from them, far, far away!" Some of us stay in bed with the blankets pulled over our heads, others self-medicate with drugs and alcohol, still others pour themselves into work so they don't have to feel.

The only problem is that the uncomfortable emotions have nowhere to go; they're still within us. We cannot push them away because they are unable to leave our minds. In pushing and struggling with them, we treat them like enemies and give energy to the distress they cause. It's like sending hate to a cloud of negative energy; the cloud just absorbs the hate and grows bigger.

In a collection of aphorisms Franz Kafka wrote, "You can hold back from the suffering of the world, you have permission to do so, and it is in accordance with your nature, but perhaps this very holding back is the one suffering you could have avoided."

Rumi continued in his poem, "Still, treat each guest honorably. He may be clearing you out for some new delight." The truth is, the difficult moments in our lives can actually be our greatest teachers and sources of growth.

Your work up to this point has been in service of giving you the tools and ability to relate to your difficulties in a radically different way. You can now see the space between stimulus and response, and you have the tools to widen that space and prime your mind for good and bolster your resiliency during difficult moments.

Life is full of difficult moments, and we all feel vulnerable at times. What if instead of wanting to get away from uncomfortable feelings, you see them as helping you get connected to the now? What if they move you into a space of awareness in which you recognized a choice point?

As you enter into the following pages, you'll learn ways to use your difficult feelings as supports instead of enemies. You'll find ways to create spaciousness around things that are uncomfortable so they don't sweep you away. You'll see that you can befriend your fear instead of running from it, drop your anxiety over your imperfections, turn anger into something constructive, and find joy within your sorrow.

What you may have thought was your enemy can now become your teacher.

45

WELCOME YOUR PAIN

Freedom is what you do with what's been done to you.

—JEAN-PAUL SARTRE

When I was six years old, my parents brought me and my two sisters into the living room, and before I had any clue what was going on, both of my sisters burst into tears. My parents proceeded to tell us that they were getting a divorce and from now on we would be living in two separate places. I stood there blankly. Concerned by my stoic reaction, my mom came up to me and asked, "What's wrong, Elisha, do you know what's going on?" To which I angrily replied, "Yeah, I know, what do you want me to do, bang my head against the wall so I'll cry?" I hadn't a clue what to do with the anger and confusion inside me, so I expressed it with willfulness.

At that time we didn't have much money, but we would occasionally go out to dinner. Even as a six-year-old, I didn't think we should be going out to dinner, and often the way I dealt with my anger was by hiding under the table and refusing to eat. My anger was not about the money but about my perception that it was wrong and unfair that our family had been torn apart. Now that I have my own kids, I look back on that time and have a lot of empathy for my parents. What do you do with a six-year-old who refuses to eat and hides defiantly under the table?

Years later, my wife noticed that whenever I got angry, I would shut down emotionally and get busy cleaning the house, washing the dishes, or checking out on the computer. If I was sitting with her, often my mind would go blank and my body would go numb. One day when I was in therapy the same thing occurred, and my therapist asked, "Elisha, where are you? It's like you're still hiding under the table." That phrase dropped me into a space of clarity. She was absolutely right. I saw that little boy inside, frightened and angry, feeling unsafe. I was freed by the realization because I was no longer controlled by my typical reaction to anger. There was now a space between me and the little boy, and in that space my heart softened. I felt a sense of compassion for my child self, and in that space I let him know that I was here and it was all going to be okay. I notice such spaces a lot more now, and often in the same moment that anger is triggered, compassion seems to gracefully arise. This is the Now Effect at work.

Sarah was a client who developed a severe case of panic attacks after having children. She reached a point where she didn't want to leave her house because everything "out there" might trigger another attack. In essence, she was hiding under the table. After we worked together, she was able to acknowledge and label the physical sensations of anxiety as they arose. This helped her recognize the space between her awareness and the discomfort. She began to change her view of the feeling from something she needed to flee from into a support to help guide her into the now. It helped her realize that she was not her anxiety but something much more. Step by step, she continued to approach instead of avoid her uncomfortable feelings, holding them within a greater space of awareness, and eventually they stopped having the same triggering effect.

As she practiced, she forged new memories and experiences of moving through difficult moments with grace. She realized that she could learn to "be with" her uncomfortable feelings instead of try-ing to fight against them and that eventually they would pass. We might say that she changed her top-down processing so that the brain no longer labeled the anxious experience as a threat but rather as something that could be approached and worked with. We may all know this intellectually, but that doesn't change the snap judgments that lie beneath our conscious awareness. To change the automatic processing of our minds, we need to give our brain new experiences to draw upon.

Now Sarah sees her panic attacks as a gift. They exposed her to a new world of learning how to be more kind and present to herself and others. She feels more confident and trusts that she can handle her anxiety with a greater sense of ease and calm. In her case, her sorrows led to joys.

Noticing how you hide under the table and joining yourself under the table with support and love allows you to come out from under-neath it into a life of emotional intelligence, healing, and freedom.

now moment

Ask yourself how you hide under the table. Write down a list of what-ever comes to mind. Is it uncomfortable to engage in certain relationships? Do you avoid certain projects because they put pressure on your mind and body? What would it be like to use the emotion as a reminder that you have entered into a choice point and experiment with Rumi's words of welcoming joys and sorrows?

As a difficulty arises, check where it is in your body and say, "Breathing in, I feel the anger, breathing out, I welcome what's here."

Check in right now to notice if seeing emotions as a support to bring you into the present moment brings up any physical or emotional discomfort. Make a mental note to practice welcoming what is there and relating to it with kindness. As you do so, you are present in a space of awareness, cultivating a trust that everything will be okay and opening the door for the gifts to reveal themselves.

www.youtube.com/NowEffect

46

THE COMMITTEE IN YOUR MIND

Imagine that there is a "committee" made up of all the various aspects of your personality sitting around a table in your mind. Though everyone on the committee is looking out for your best interests, they all have their opinions about what that means. Now imagine that sitting at one end of the table is a wounded person, a part of you that others on the committee see as a threat, a "weak link," and try their best to either ignore or judge harshly in the hope that it will be driven away.

The problem is that there are no doors to the committee room, so those personalities are stuck there. Imagine that the wounded being is a little part of you. How is it feeling? The response I usually get from people I work with is "insecure," "not well," or "hurt."

The more the other committee members ignore and judge, the more that wounded committee member feels that she doesn't belong, that something is wrong with her, and her energy is dragged down into deeper cycles of shame, anger, or fear.

When I ask people, "If you had a good friend who was feeling any of those things, how would ignoring or rejecting the friend be helpful in her healing?"

The answer is often "It would make her feel worse." So I follow with "What would be helpful for this friend?" The answer is usually "Taking care of her," "Being with her," or "Giving her a hug."

I then say, "That is exactly what that committee member (your feelings) needs."

When you treat the wounded, scared, or shamed part of yourself with compassion, it sends the message that you care enough about yourself to be with yourself; it also begins to demonstrate to your subconscious mind, through experience, that you don't always have to run from your difficult emotions.

In order to be a healthy, well-integrated person, everyone on the committee needs to feel accepted, loved, and understood, including the ones who feel shame and the ones who fear the shame.

The committee needs a leader, a CEO, that can help guide everyone toward understanding that when one member feels threatened, it hinders the collective energy. This leader, which is your wise mind, can emerge only when you notice the space between your awareness and the committee. In this space you can gain perspective, see that the committee has been ostracizing a part of you, and choose to bring a beginner's mind to the pain, attending with empathy and compassion, bringing it back into the fold, and breaking the cycle of feeling stuck.

now moment

Can you identify a part of you that you wish wasn't there? That would be something you're ashamed of, that you actively judge or wish was different. That is the committee ganging up against that part of yourself. Bring awareness to that part; what does it need? As much as the majority of the committee in your mind would like to get away from it or get rid of it, often what it needs most is to be understood and cared for. The moment you recognize that part of yourself is the moment you step into a space of awareness where you're relating *to* the pain instead of *from* the pain.

Herein lies the choice point where you can take the first step to pay attention to it, without judgment and with mindfulness. The second step is to make contact with it, to find out where the feeling is embodied, where it hurts, and use it as a support to bring you here. Do you experience it as a heaviness in your chest or heart or as a constriction in your stomach or neck? Place your hands gently on your heart and offer care to this woundedness.

Practice "Breathing in, may I feel safe and protected, breathing out, may I be free from suffering."

47

BEFRIEND YOUR FEAR

Love is what we were born with. Fear is what we learned here.   —MARIANNE WILLIAMSON

n 1967 a young college student named Jack Kornfield shifted his focus at Dartmouth College from organic chemistry to Buddhist and Asian studies partly because he was looking for answers to how to heal the fear he was carrying from past traumas of growing up in a family with a violent and abusive father. When I asked him about this, he said, "My father was so full of rage, I didn't want to be like him. Lo and behold, I discovered that it [rage] was not just in him but was in me as well." Though fear may stem from our memories of yesterday and be fueled by anticipation of the future, it actually occurs right now. Over the years Jack became aware of how the stories he held in his mind influenced the way he saw life and how he carried the trauma and fear in his body. From this space of awareness he was able to begin his practice toward achieving mindfulness, compassion, and a wise heart that paved the way for healing.

Fear is a part of human experience. It is not good or bad; a little fear can motivate us to make change, while a lot of fear can create a reaction that leaves us paralyzed, panicked, or feeling overwhelmed.

But as Rumi says, "No matter how fast you run, your shadow more than keeps up."

Some people consider fear to be at the root of every problem. It draws on past life lessons and experiences to make us perceive that something is to be guarded against right now, even when there is no real danger.

I've seen people who continue to fight with their partners, not because they actually think there will be a resolution, but because they perceive a threat of being controlled as they were as a child.

I've seen people who are afraid to go out on dates, not for lack of prospects, but because their mind is protecting them against the painful feeling of rejection that they experienced while growing up or in past relationships.

I've seen people who are afraid to let go of control in their relationships or environments because they couldn't control the death of a loved one.

I've seen wealthy workaholics who see that their families are suffering in their absence but who won't cut down on their work hours because of an irrational fear of becoming financially poor, as they were when they were children.

I've seen people who have been depressed, who, although they have new tools to work with their emotions, won't allow themselves to feel sad out of fear that it will drag them back into the deep depression they experienced before.

Fear is powerful, and we're very loyal to it because it promises to be our protector, but in fact it subtly becomes our captor. The underlying current of it can keep us trapped in ruminating on traumas from the past that color the present moment and anticipating the future, keeping us further away from the Now Effect.

When working with fear, Jack discovered that "you have to do it a little bit at a time. As you befriend your fear, you say, 'Oh, this is fear.'" This is equivalent to "If you can name it, you can tame it" or creating the GABA bath, showering the "fear circuit" in your brain. We will now take this a step further.

As you use fear as a support to ground you in the present moment, it can become a choice point to turn toward your fear and pay attention to it with a kind eye. When dealing with your fear, you will understand that it is possible to be present and that awareness and compassion are bigger than fear. You can achieve a shift away from being lost in the fear to being present and compassionate with your insecurity. When we accept our vulnerability, we open in a way that allows for a wise and much more fully lived life.

now moment

Can you identify any areas of your personal life or work where you experience being afraid? Take a moment to really picture and think about this. What stories does your fear tell, and how does it manifest in your body? Befriend your fear. Recognize fear as it arises, see it as a choice point, expand the space, and say, "Oh, this is fear." Notice the story your fear is telling and where it is in the body each time it arises.

As you notice fear, you can reconnect with your heart. Practice "Breathing in, I feel the fear, breathing out, I hold it with a heart of compassion."

48

THE ANXIOUS TRAVELER

Anne long enjoyed the traveling she did for work. With all the miles she racked up she was treated like royalty. Getting on the plane was like entering a space of free time. There were no responsibilities and she could just relax, flip through a magazine, listen to music, or watch an entertaining movie. But a short flight from LAX to SFO on August 4, 2010, changed all of that. "We're all going to die" was the first thing she remembered another passenger yelling as the person in the seat next to her grabbed her arm. The turbulence was intense and had been that way for ten minutes. The flight attendants were trying to assure everyone that things were going to be okay as they hurriedly made their way back to their seats to buckle up. Anne began to white-knuckle the arms of her chair. *"Where's the voice of the captain telling us what's going on?"* Anne thought. *"Who's in control here?"* Twenty minutes later the plane made a jerky landing, everyone was safe, but that's not the story Anne's mind told her.

She had become an anxious traveler, and she thought she'd never be able to fly again.

We've all heard the adage "It is what it is," but I like to add another piece saying, "It is what it is, *while it is.*"

This speaks to a larger reality that whatever exists is impermanent, including our fear. When automatic thoughts of panic and worry begin creeping into your mind, saying "it is what it is, while it is" pops you out of autopilot, into the present moment, and reminds you that this feeling is impermanent. This reminder helps you to not get so wrapped up in it and can give you the choice to do a short mindfulness practice to calm your body and be kinder to yourself.

This phrase was enormously helpful for Anne in nipping her worries in the bud and expanding her space of awareness to choose how she wanted to approach the situation. Recognizing the impermanence of the feeling allowed her to feel safer about becoming curious about her fear. As she did this, she transformed from feeling out of control with fear to feeling in control of her fear.

Once you've calmed down the emotional brain you can engage the rational brain and remind yourself of the fact that far more people get killed in car accidents every year than in plane crashes. Or that you may have a greater chance at being killed by a bolt of lightning than being in a plane crash.

As you practice this phrase as an anxious traveler you might also realize that you can use it for positive situations. Recognizing the impermanence of a good feeling can lead you to appreciate it more.

now moment

Take this moment to recognize how you're feeling right now. Say to yourself, "It is what it is, while it is." See if you can stay with the feeling and notice it change in small ways right before your eyes. Now bring this into your day and into your travels.

49

YOU ARE IMPERFECT
JUST AS YOU ARE

Fred was a thirty-eight-year-old businessman who originally came to see me to seek support for depression. He was respected, climbing up the corporate ladder, and receiving accolades from his colleagues for all his good work. On the outside, he was the guy everyone wanted to be; people said he had the golden touch. However, on the inside the weather couldn't have been more different. He believed his success was like a house of cards that could come crashing down at any moment because, in his mind, he was a fake, and somehow he had been fooling people for a long time. He also had a general mistrust of any compliments that came his way. There was a voice inside his head that told him something was wrong, he didn't belong, and soon people would find out.

One day I was writing in a local coffee shop, and Fred walked by on his way to work. After deliberating whether it was appropriate to approach me or not, he came up to me, smiled, and said, "Hi, Elisha." I was genuinely happy to see him and got up, gave him a hug, and told him to have a good day. I immediately wondered whether

I should have given him a hug, as it's generally not traditional to do so in a therapist-patient relationship, but it felt like the right thing to do. The following week when Fred came in, he said, "I want to first thank you for the hug. You see, up until this point I just had this thought in my mind that you thought I was a defect and despised me, and after that hug I felt how you cared for me and that thought just melted away."

The stories that cycle in our minds can be the purveyors of so much pain. Fred suffers from the "something is wrong with me" syndrome. It's not an issue that has made it into the *Diagnostic and Statistical Manual of Mental Disorders* (*DSM*) yet, but it is probably one of the most widespread. The author, psychologist, and meditation teacher Tara Brach accurately calls this the "Trance of Unworthiness."

From some source—family, society, the media—we have received and internalized the message that we're defective, deficient, and imperfect.

What is it that produces this feeling of unworthiness and shame for so many of us? What past stories or wounds are creating this perception? Some of us started taking in the story of our unworthiness when we were young and felt we had to be perfect to get positive attention or love from our parents. Others became enthralled by the media's airbrushed pictures of models showing us what a "normal" body looks like. For others it might have been the billboards and commercials showing how happy children were when they had a particular expensive toy that we didn't have.

The Japanese Zen Buddhist Dōgen Zenji said, "To be in harmony with the wholeness of things is not to have anxiety over imperfections." The news flash is that we are *all* imperfect, and that is okay. Accepting ourselves as imperfect doesn't mean that we should become complacent and not make plans or not take action to achieve mental and physical health. It simply means operating from the perspective that we are all imperfect, so we can begin practicing kindness, instead of fear and hate, toward our imperfections when they arise.

now moment

Is there a part of you that believes that something is wrong with you, or is there something that you feel ashamed or embarrassed about? Take a moment to think about what that is, and then practice these three steps to begin making peace with your imperfections, cultivating compassion and realizing greater emotional freedom.

1. ACCEPT. The first step is to accept the fact that you are as imperfect as the rest of us.

2. SEE THE AUTOMATIC NEGATIVE THOUGHT (ANT). In Part III, "Know Your Mind, Change Your Brain," you learned how cognitive therapists refer to our automatic negative thoughts as ANTs in our minds. ANTs may arise out of fear: "Yes, but I have many more imperfections than most people." This may be a committee member trying to keep you safe from disappointment, but in the process the thought keeps you stuck. If ANTs arise, notice them as automatic negative thoughts (because that is what they are), let them be, and bring your attention to the following step.

3. REPARENT WITH KINDNESS. Bring kindness to the moment. Bring your attention to the feeling that you are experiencing right now, and use it as a support to become present. You may feel a sense of vulnerability, shame, disgust, fear, sadness, or anger.

Put both hands where the feeling arises in the body, and take a moment to experience your hands' warmth and pressure. Now imagine the feeling as a little baby, maybe yourself as an infant or a child. Say to this part of yourself, "I care about your pain, and I love you just the way you are." Or use whatever other words work for you.

Note: Be aware of any judgments that arise while you are doing this exercise, such as "This is a waste of time" or "I could never do this." These ANTs are habitual mind patterns that have been with you for quite some time. They may be caused by a committee member that's afraid to approach what is difficult and therefore judges it in an effort to keep you away. When this happens, notice it and bring your attention back to reparenting the pain with kindness.

Practice "Breathing in, I open myself to what's vulnerable, breathing out, I let go of the need to be perfect."

50

YOUR JOY IS
YOUR SORROW UNMASKED

It takes both sunshine and rain to make a rainbow.

—PROVERB

Roberto Assagioli was born in Venice, Italy, to a middle-class Jewish family. In 1938 Benito Mussolini's government imprisoned Assagioli because of his Jewish heritage and his writings on human values. During his month in solitary confinement he spent the time in deep reflection and meditation about what it truly means to be human. Through the process of stepping into his sorrow while imprisoned he found wells of love, wisdom, and joy. He later came to develop the theory of psychosynthesis, which says that when we spend time avoiding uncomfortable emotions we also close ourselves off to more comfortable ones. In essence, we live by adopting a "survival personality," restricting our emotional capacity, and simply getting by from day to day. When we allow ourselves to open up to the difficult, we also open up to the fullness of life.

From Assagioli's perspective, we can think of how we experience emotions through three levels. On the top level are comfortable emotions such as joy, courage, and love, and on the bottom are uncomfortable emotions like fear, anger, and sadness. The middle level represents our survival personality, a restricted area safe from the sorrow but also barred from the joy. In order to expand the center area and reach the joy, we must also be able to experience the sorrow.

A few years ago, on a cloudy day, I was walking in Shoreline Park in Mountain View, California, experiencing deep sadness after having heard that a family friend had just passed away. My mind started swimming with thoughts about my family and what would happen if my wife died, and I began to cry. In that moment I sat down, closed my eyes, and felt a natural inclination to step down from the story in my mind and connect with the physical feeling of sadness, just being with it. As I opened my eyes, I saw a lake in front of me and thought, *"That is beautiful."* A feeling of peace came over me, and although the sadness was still there, it felt like a sweet sorrow. Being with the feeling of sorrow, I found the feeling of joy and sensed that everything was going to be okay.

now moment

Where does sadness arise in your life? Do you allow yourself to feel it, or do you quickly become distracted? What would it be like to dip your toes in it when it arises, exploring how it feels, the texture and the shape of it? If there is sorrow present right now, take a moment to gently bring awareness to the texture of the feeling. By becoming familiar with sorrow, you can be better able to appreciate joy and you may open the doors to a wise heart.

51

YOUR ACE IN THE HOLE

Whenever you fall, pick something up.

—OSWALD AVERY

Depression struck Alice at thirteen and ruined the quality of her life for the next forty years. Every day was a murky maze of underlying negative thoughts and painful feelings that attacked her like viruses. She tried everything she could, including drinking and smoking, to hide out or get numb and escape the barrage of negativity that filled her mind. Alice entered into Mindfulness-Based Cognitive Therapy (MBCT), an eight-week program during which she systematically trained her mind to come down from the automatic negative thoughts and into her body and to redirect her actions toward things that gave her a sense of achievement. After the program she said there was a key practice that she carried with her to help open the spaces of her life and make a change: the ACE practice.

Alice teaches high school in South Central Los Angeles to teenagers who are often angry and depressed. It's challenging, as they repeatedly act out and sometimes curse at her in the middle of class. In the past she would hurl a sarcastic remark at them, which only made them angrier. But now that she has primed her mind to do the ACE practice and reset the button they've pushed, she is able to act and respond to them from a place of composure and balance.

When you practice ACE, you are continuing to plant Now Effect seeds in your garden. You may not see the plant grow immediately, but know that you are nurturing it in your mind.

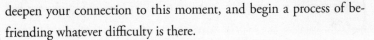

now moment

ACE is an acronym that I taught Alice in the MBCT course to prevent depressive relapse. Whether you've experienced depression or not, this practice can be used to break out of autopilot, steady your mind, deepen your connection to this moment, and begin a process of befriending whatever difficulty is there.

www.youtube.com/NowEffect

- A: AWARENESS of your thoughts, feelings, and sensations. For example, you may notice worried thoughts about an upcoming vacation and be feeling anxious. This feeling is expressed in your body as a rapid heartbeat or a constriction in the chest. Or maybe there is looseness and a sense of calmness and your thoughts are moving more slowly. The purpose of awareness is to break out of autopilot and come into the now.
- C: COLLECTING your attention to your breath. In this practice we're not simply taking a few deep breaths; instead, we're allowing our attention to rest easily on the natural rhythms of the breath. You

might choose to see where you notice the breath most prominently. Is it at the tip of the nose, in the chest, or in the stomach? During this practice your mind will wander to all its stories, and that is perfectly fine. Play with your attention, knowing that there's no need to judge the wandering mind. Instead, you can practice "See, touch, go," bringing curiosity to where it wandered and in that space of awareness choose a different response—to gently bring your mind and attention back to the breath.

E: EXPANDING your attention throughout your entire body. This is different from naming how your body is feeling. It is training your mind to be with what is happening now and is another way to accept the reality of what is here and letting it be. Sadness may be expressed as heaviness in the face or chest, anger may be seen in a tightening of your muscles, fear may be felt in a rapid heartbeat. Bring a beginner's mind to the feeling, along with kind attention.

Start off by practicing ACE for just a few minutes right now. After the practice, reflect on what you noticed during the space you created. What's most important to pay attention to right now? Maybe it's making a phone call to a friend or family member you've been putting off. Or perhaps it's putting a few daily practice reminders in your calendar to begin sowing the seeds of the Now Effect. If you are not experiencing a difficulty at the moment, you can still give this practice a try. Just engaging in the practice plants a seed in your memory, making it more likely to recall during difficult moments.

If your mind comes up with a story of how now isn't the right time to do ACE and you tell yourself that you'll get to it later, simply see the net effect of that thought. Notice the thought, and see if it's rooted in avoidance and keeping you further from realizing the Now Effect.

ANGER: CONSTRUCTIVE, DESTRUCTIVE, OR BOTH?

If you are patient in one moment of anger, you will escape
one hundred days of sorrow.   —CHINESE PROVERB

At some point in my late teenage years a shift happened within me and I developed an uncanny ability to calm myself in moments of anger. It was as if when the anger arose, my system shut down and I was completely cut off from it. I held a belief that anger was an ineffective emotion and didn't help any situation and there was really no point in expressing it. Years later I came to understand that emotions aren't always so black and white and that my anger was mixed up with feelings of sadness and shame. The feeling was overwhelming, so when anger arose my mind made the snap judgment to nip it in the bud by telling me it was destructive. When I met my wife, there were many times when she would become frustrated with me because when I felt anger, I would shut down and disconnect from her. I'd say, "What's the point of getting angry and shouting? What good will that do?" I was, yet again, hiding under the table. Disconnecting from anger also kept me from being assertive and standing up for myself when anyone said something that was hurtful. As I continued to deny this natural human emotion, I reinforced a cycle of shame, constantly feeling as though something was wrong with me when I got angry. What I didn't realize was that I was confusing the emotion of anger with the act of aggression.

There is absolutely nothing wrong with feeling or expressing anger. Whenever we're frustrated, irritated, or annoyed we are experiencing a form of anger. We can be angry due to a myriad of things, from our partners making plans for us without asking to being abused as a child. It's how we express the anger that makes the difference.

The psychologist and author of *Destructive Emotions: A Scientific Dialogue with the Dalai Lama,* Daniel Goleman, PhD, wrote that expressing anger can be positive. Outrage over injustice moves us to help others. Anger about the atrocities in Darfur has spurred international support; anger over being abused may lead to the cry for help; a teenager's anger over Mom or Dad opening the bedroom door without knocking may lead to a discussion about boundaries. There is a way to be assertive without being aggressive when we are angry. But first we need to be aware of the anger, see it as a choice point to be less reactive, and respond in a skillful, compassionate way. Goleman calls this "constructive anger."

Phil Jackson is arguably the most accomplished NBA basketball coach of all time, having led the Chicago Bulls and Los Angeles Lakers to many championships. He is also known as the "Zen master" among his followers. He taught his basketball teams mindfulness as a means of helping them, as he puts it, "stay calm and centered (well, most of the time)" in the midst of a game. If you've ever watched basketball or any other sport, you have seen how easy it is for coaches and players to fly off the handle at a referee's call they don't agree with. In his book *Sacred Hoops,* Jackson said, "During games I often get agitated by bad calls, but years of meditation practice have taught me how to find that still point within me so I can argue passionately with the refs without being overwhelmed by anger."

Some of us are comfortable with expressing anger; others have been traumatized by anger in the past. Perhaps you never had a role model who expressed anger constructively, or maybe you resonate with my story of anger being mixed up with other uncomfortable emotions, leading you to disconnect from it entirely. The problem is that when we feel anger and attempt to bottle it up, it's like an active volcano: it will erupt as irritability, depression, distress, or aggression. Pent-up anger and resentment can kill a relationship.

Aggression or hostility is often destructive and causes the person on the receiving end to go into fight-or-flight mode, either shutting down or responding with aggression. Either way, the results are usually less than optimal. Research shows us that acts of aggression fuel the fire for more aggression. So although smashing plates on the floor can offer small moments of relief, it doesn't do anything to heal the anger. Learning to become aware of the space between the stimulus and response can provide us with the possibility of shifting our reaction from destructive to constructive.

now moment

Make your anger constructive. Consider something that made you angry. You don't need to choose your angriest moment, just one that fueled frustration, irritation, or annoyance. Picture the scene as if it were a movie. What was happening? What was the worst part about it? Where did you feel the anger in your body? Were there any mind traps, such as exaggerating the negative and discounting the positive? As you fully imagine the scene, take a moment to pause and breathe. Can you acknowledge your anger without judgment? Anger is not good or bad, right or wrong; it is simply an emotion that you are experiencing. As you allow the feeling to support you in becoming present, you may find that underneath the anger is sadness or another emotion. By practicing with a past event, you can teach yourself to find the space to acknowledge your anger when you are in the moment. Another technique that can help externalize what you're feeling is to write it down. Capturing your feelings on paper can help stop the spiraling of your mind.

As you practice focusing on your anger, know that you are the best judge of your limits. If the feelings are too strong, you can STOP and come back to this exercise another time with a less triggering event.

part VII

GETTING CONNECTED

In 2005 I conducted a national research study to determine whether people could cultivate more sacred moments in their lives and, if so, what was the effect and essence of their experience. I found that people were able to do so and that what was so precious about those moments was a sense of connection.

As human beings, we are wired for connection. Every one of us has a chemical in our brains called oxytocin that surges when we feel connected (for example, a mother breast-feeding her child, a friend hugging you, a loved one gazing into your eyes). Oxytocin creates a feeling of contentment that makes us want to connect again.

It's an evolutionary necessity to feel that we belong, that we are not alone. Research shows that the more quality relationships you have, the greater your contentment, the lower your stress, and the longer your life.

The problem is, our culture makes it very difficult to achieve that feeling. Mother Teresa said, "The biggest disease today is not leprosy or tuberculosis but rather the feeling of not belonging." She spent her adult life with people who were ostracized by society; she knew better than most the pain of not being part of a community. Our minds seem to be drawn to our differences more than our commonalities. And what seems different or alien to us often fuels our fears and causes us to oppress and segregate.

Up to this point in *The Now Effect* we've been focusing mainly on connecting to ourselves. In the following section we're going to broaden what we've learned and bring it to our relationships and the rest of the world.

THE BIGGEST DISEASE

We may all have come in different ships, but we're in the same boat now. —MARTIN LUTHER KING, JR.

Father Gregory Boyle spends his life working in neighborhoods with the highest concentration of murderous gang activity. His mission is to cultivate a sense of kinship in those communities. He reminds us that this happens when we remember that we belong to one another. In his book *Tattoos on the Heart* he wrote, "I suspect that were kinship our goal, we would no longer be promoting justice—we would be celebrating it."

In my experience, we have the best chance of making change in our lives when we feel connected and supported by an active community. For thousands of years people have been gathering in churches, synagogues, mosques, temples, sports stadiums, and convention centers to come together and share common interests, goals, and values.

This isn't an accident; it's because we have a natural inclination to gather with like-minded people and feel that we belong.

How can we create a community when we engage in our everyday relationships on autopilot and automatically judge people without seeing past the label we put on them? As you may have guessed, the secret is in the spaces we create by living the Now Effect.

Learning to recognize the spaces of awareness in our lives extends beyond the individual. We can transform our relationships when we realize the interconnectedness of all human beings and recognize the spaces of awareness in relationships.

We can start to see the spaces between the moment we encounter another person and our immediate judgment of them. This knee-jerk judgment can happen when we meet someone for the first time, or it can emerge when dealing with a colleague, spouse, or friend. But we can intentionally dissolve the delusion of disconnection and the top-down processing that lumps that person in with prior experiences and actually see the person.

The result is better communication, stronger relationships, a greater sense of security and belonging, more compassion, and increased happiness.

now moment

In the Zulu tribe in southern Africa, when two people meet, one person says, "I am here," and the other answers, "I see you." Here are three steps you can try out with anyone you come into contact with today to move from the default of disconnection to the intention of connection.

1. PUT ASIDE YOUR LENSES OF JUDGMENT AND *SEE THE PERSON*. Whether you believe it or not, you instantly judge someone as soon as you see him or her. You may make assumptions about people based on the color of their skin, their ethnicity, a memory you have of them, or the expressions on their faces. This is someone who has a history of adventures, failures, loves, fears, regrets, triumphs, hurts, losses, traumas, family, and friends—just like you. See if you can set judgment aside for a moment and adopt fresh eyes. See this person as if for the very first time.

2. ASK YOURSELF, "WHAT DOES THIS PERSON MOST DEEPLY WANT?" The answer is within you, and it most likely has something to do with being treated kindly and feeling a sense of belonging.

3. GIVE A GESTURE THAT FEEDS THAT NEED. Smile at the person; ask her if you can help; listen to what he has to say; if she is a family member or friend, tell her you love her.

When relating to another person, we can always ask ourselves if what we are doing is in the service of connection or disconnection. It's a simple question that can sometimes lead to important answers and actions.

The fact is, when we or others around us feel understood and cared about, a sense of acceptance and belonging arises. This breaks down barriers and makes relationships better.

54

DISCONNECTION IS DELUSION

Somewhere along the way, many of us develop the notion that the goal of life is for us, individually, to be happy. To achieve this, we begin to focus on ourselves and exclude others. The eighth-century Indian scholar Shantideva said, "All joy in this world comes from wanting others to be happy, and all suffering in this world comes from wanting only oneself to be happy."

The fact is, we are not islands, and we are far more connected than we know.

In 1951 the quantum physicist David Bohm developed quantum theory, which brought to light the science behind our interconnectedness. He said that if you were able to separate an atomic particle into two elements and send each to opposite ends of the world, changing the spin of one would instantly change the spin of the other. This proves that although we may feel separate and alone, we are all interconnected. This is no different from what many spiritual traditions have been saying for millennia.

Consider the fact that as I write these words and you read them, the energy from my thoughts that I put out in the past is now weaving into the neural pathways of your brain and changing them. In this moment, across time, there is an energy flowing between us. We are connected.

Many of us walk around feeling disconnected, alone, and in the default narrative of *me*. There is no question that we all have unique histories, individually and culturally, but if we could realize that beyond our perception of separateness there is a much deeper level of connection, we might choose to intentionally put out kinder and more compassionate energy. At the end of the day, engaging in this manner feeds our most primal need to love and feel loved.

now moment

www.youtube.com/NowEffect

Think of all the different people out there—people of different classes who live in different countries, have different skin tones, follow different religions. Hold those people in your mind, and practice a phrase created by the Stanford psychologist and neuroscientist Philippe Goldin, PhD: "Just like me." Take this phrase with you today, and whenever you notice yourself passing someone whom you judge as different from you, say to yourself, "Just like me." As you do so, does it influence how you see those other people? Does it change the way you respond to them?

Try acting out of the deep knowledge that we are all truly connected. Breathing in, slide underneath your judgments and feel the connection with humanity; breathing out, let go of the delusion of disconnection.

Practice "Breathing in, I see you, breathing out, you're just like me."

THE SCIENCE OF CONNECTION

It's not earth-shattering news that the people we surround ourselves with influence how we feel, what we think, what we wear, and how we eat. But what about our larger circle of friends of friends of friends? The social scientists Nicholas Christakis, MD, PhD, and James Fowler, PhD, conducted a study to look at the effect of social networks. To determine if there was a causal relationship with obesity, they mapped the relationships of 12,067 people who had more than 50,000 connections to other people that were assessed repeatedly from 1971 to 2003 (not online social networks such as Facebook but physical networks of people). They found that, indeed, "birds of a feather flock together." However, they found something much more interesting: obesity doesn't start and stop with immediate friends and family; it is "contagious" by up to three degrees of separation.

It's not that there is a physiological contagion, as with a cold, but behaviors do seem to be "catching." The *New Yorker* writer Malcolm Gladwell is probably most responsible for popularizing this concept in *The Tipping Point,* where he said, "Ideas and products and messages and behaviors spread just like viruses do." So if people around you eat poorly, you will pick up on the idea, message, or feeling that junk food goes with lunch, and you will eat the pounds on. Staying healthy is a product not only of our individual will but of our proximity and connections to other healthy people.

Christakis and Fowler took this investigation further to study the possibility of "emotional contagion" and found that loneliness also spreads three degrees. In the paper "Alone in the Crowd: The Structure and Spread of Loneliness in a Large Social Network," published in 2009 with John Cacioppo, PhD, they said, "The spread of loneliness was found to be stronger than the spread of perceived social connections, stronger for friends than family members, and stronger for women than for men."

They explained that "the spread of good or bad feelings might be driven partly by 'mirror neurons' in the brain that automatically mimic what we see in the faces of those around us—which is why looking at photographs of smiling people can itself often lift your mood." So if there are people in your network who are having difficulties in their lives, your brain may begin to mimic their mood.

Christakis and Fowler also found that happiness spreads by three degrees of separation and each additional person in your life who is feeling well boosts your chances of feeling well by 9 percent.

The science behind connection reveals that the practices and writings you are engaging in to change your own life have a far greater effect than on your life alone. As you begin to play with the spaces of awareness, the idea of the practice will begin to spread to your friends of friends of friends, who will go on to affect their friends of friends of friends, and so on.

When carbon atoms are arranged in a specific way, they make a diamond, but the diamond is not in each carbon atom. In the same way, each of our roles in mindfully engaging life can create a social effect that is greater than each of us alone, having a significant influence on shaping our culture for the years to come and providing enormous healing.

Who is in your immediate social network? Are they supportive of your work to become more present to your life? If so, great! If not, is there a way you can get in touch with others who live in accordance with those values? Maybe there are people on the periphery of your life whom you can reconnect with, or maybe you can look online for interest groups that meet in your area that support these practices. What would life be like if you surrounded yourself with people who were supportive of your living the life you want?

WHY ARE YOU WAITING?

If you wish to experience peace, provide peace for another.

—THE DALAI LAMA

At 5:30 AM Roger's alarm jolted him out of bed. He immediately checked his cell phone for work and personal messages that he could get caught up on before the day began. On his voice mail was a message from his mom, whom he'd been avoiding for a few months because of an argument. He loved her, but withholding his love was a way of getting back at her for hurting him. Anyway, he had other things to worry about, such as his health. But looking at his watch, he realized he was running late for work; exercising would have to wait until tomorrow.

On that sunny morning of September 11, 2001, after showering and grabbing a breakfast bar, he left his Fifth Avenue apartment in New York and began walking toward his office in the World Trade Center. He looked up and saw the first plane crash into one of the towers. As the building shook and swayed and flames ripped through the air, Roger, along with millions of others, was jolted into a giant space of awareness, realizing that whom you love and how you love them is what's really important and the rest of it never mattered.

The weight of the fight with his mom disappeared in the moments that followed as Roger picked up his phone and made the call he'd been putting off.

Why does it often take a catastrophic event to shake us into the now and connect us to what and who is most important? After Mitch Albom, author of *Tuesdays with Morrie,* found out that his former professor Morrie Schwartz was dying of Lou Gehrig's disease, he spent every Tuesday with him. In the process he learned that in this life you must get back in touch with how to love yourself and those around you.

We seem to go through life in a trance, with brief moments of clarity. One reason we become so mind-blind to the preciousness of each moment is that we have a habit of denying life's impermanence. Many people don't want to talk about dying. Woody Allen once said, "I don't mind dying as long as I don't have to be there." Death makes most people uncomfortable, but the mind does something very interesting with this information: it banishes it to remote corners of the brain so we become unaware of our own unawareness of our mortality or the preciousness of life. That can be a mind twister, and we may need to read it over a few times.

Many of us have waking moments when we feel the importance of our relationships, and reading this chapter may have ignited one of those moments, but more often than not, we soon fall back asleep, over and over again.

We don't have to wait for a crisis to bring us to clarity. The good news is that we have the ability to connect to who really matters right now.

Who in your life have you been disconnected from or been meaning to call or make contact with? What's holding you back—fear, anger, shame? Or is it that you've been swept up into your routine and don't have the time? Now is the time to make time. Make a plan in this space of awareness to drop a note, make a call, or make a date to see the person. Though your overture may not be met with the response you desire, remember that you can control only your own behavior and making the effort is what is important right now.

57

BROTHER BRUNO AND THE FROG

There is an old folktale of a man named Brother Bruno. While he was in meditation one night, he heard a bullfrog croaking outside and disturbing his ability to concentrate. He tried to ignore the sound, but to no avail. Finally, he opened his window and shouted, "Quiet! I'm meditating!"

Because Brother Bruno held the status of saint, all living creatures obeyed his request and fell silent. As he sat back into meditation, another sound began to bother him. This time it came from within. It was his own voice, saying, "Perhaps God is pleased with the bullfrog's croaking. Why else would he be croaking?" Another voice from within retorted, "But the voice is so distracting to my meditation, what could be pleasing about it?" To this the first voice said, "Why not listen and find out?"

Brother Bruno opened the window again, leaned out, and shouted, "Sing!" The bullfrog, along with all the other frogs, began to join in song. As Brother Bruno began to bring mindfulness to the sound of the frogs, he realized there was harmony in it. Instead of resisting the sounds that caused him suffering, bringing his attention to them enriched his experience. He felt at peace with the frogs and the sounds and realized the power of mindfulness, especially mindful listening.

So it can be with our relationships. What someone is trying to tell us, or simply his or her annoying tone of voice, may close us down. And when another person asks, "Are you listening to me?" we halfheartedly reply, "Yes, I heard every word you said." Hearing, however, is very different from listening. Hearing implies a passive reception of pitches, tones, and frequencies but no intention to understand what the other person is trying to say. Listening is an active activity, which implies paying attention to the person's words, tone of voice, and body language to receive and understand his or her message.

The truth is that we feel less defensive and more open and connected when we feel listened to because it gives us the sense that the other person is trying to understand us and cares about us. Being listened to gives us a feeling of acceptance and belonging. The foundation of any good relationship is mindful listening.

But our emotions have a clever way of subconsciously subverting our attention. If something makes us happy or reinforces our position, we listen carefully, but if something makes us unhappy or refutes our position, we are likely to hear it but not really listen.

Selective hearing has a profound effect on our relationships. We have the ability, in any space of awareness within a relationship, to notice if we're merely hearing, so we can choose to listen and create a transformative moment of connection. As you engage in this practice, focus less on the immediate outcome and more on the gradual shift of opening, empathy, and connection that occurs from moment to moment.

Brother Bruno transformed irritation into harmony; you have the power to do the same.

Think of some interactions coming up today. Are you going to be meeting with a colleague, seeing a loved one, or just interacting with someone you don't know too well? Try bringing awareness to those moments as well as the intention of mindful listening. Do so for the sole purpose of understanding and caring about the other person. He or she wants to be accepted at a deep level, just as you do.

Practice asking yourself, "Am I listening?" "Where is my mind right now?" Then take a breath and listen.

58

BUDDHA IN THE BEDROOM

One day when my wife came home from work, I was lying on the couch resting my eyes, and she started telling me about her problems from that day. The main one concerned a conflict at work with a colleague, and she was feeling frustrated. At that moment my body started to get tense, and unsolicited advice began to spout from my mouth.

During the interaction, I noticed that something didn't feel right. I felt disconnected and stuck between not saying anything and giving advice. At one point she responded, "You know, it would have been better if you were a little more curious about my experience instead of giving me advice."

At that moment, a lightbulb went off in my mind and I found there was another way I could have related to her. Now I try to bring curiosity to our relationship more often, and it has been enormously helpful. I try to check my judgments at the door, and instead of jumping to conclusions I ask, "What do you mean by that?" or "How was that for you?" or "I'm not sure I understand, tell me more."

Adopting the intention and attitude of curiosity is a cornerstone of reconnecting in any relationship. As human beings, we all want to feel understood and cared about; that is what gives us a feeling of acceptance. Curiosity communicates, "I'm interested in you, I'm paying attention, I care about you." This often allows people's guard to come down and creates the opportunity to move from disconnection to connection.

Curiosity doesn't just play a verbal role, it can also play a physical role; so if you're in a loving relationship, it may be time to bring back physical curiosity. Don't be fooled; the brain brings its top-down processing to our physical relationships too. That is why everything is so vibrant, so new, and so fresh early in a relationship. It's easy to feel connected. Our brain rewards us by turning up the oxytocin, which makes us feel good with every touch, kiss, and hug. But as time goes on the brain says, "Been there, done that," and what used to be a long embrace turns to a quick peck on the lips.

The moment you recognize you're disconnected is the moment when you have moved into a space of awareness, a choice point to get curious and move toward connection.

now moment

The following seven practices are meant as ways to weave more curiosity and connection into the spaces of your relationship and cultivate intimacy and attunement with yourself and/or another person. After reading them, choose one to do right now and get connected.

1. SET YOUR INTENTION UPON WAKING UP. Set the intention in your mind to bring curiosity into your relationship both verbally

and physically. If thoughts or judgments arise, label them as mere thoughts, and recommit to your intention.

2. HUG MINDFULLY. Try to make hugging the first thing you do when you see someone close to you. Let the hug last until you feel both bodies relax, indicating that the nervous systems have been connected. See if you can linger just a bit longer than normal, taking in the feeling of each moment.

3. SEND LOVING-KINDNESS. While at work, see if you can wish yourself and/or your significant other wishes of loving-kindness. You might say to yourself, "May you be well, safe, happy, and healthy." This is important to do even, and often especially, if you are having ill feelings toward your significant other.

4. HOLD HANDS. Whether you're on vacation or just taking a short stroll after a meal, reach out and hold each other's hands. Bring attention to the feeling of touch as you hold each other's hands. If your mind jumps in, saying, "I don't want to be one of those couples holding hands in public," just note it as a thought and give it a shot. Know you are connecting physically as you do this.

5. GAZE MINDFULLY. The eyes are one of the most intimate doorways to connection. You'll notice that when you feel disconnected, you look into the other person's eyes less. Take a few minutes to look into each other's eyes. Be aware of the color of the other person's eyes and whatever thoughts and emotions arise during this time. Share the thoughts and feelings that come up with each other.

6. SET A MINDFUL MOOD. When creating a setting to cultivate intimacy, whether you are lighting candles, putting on music, or donning special lingerie, move slightly more slowly. Pay attention to your senses. If you are lighting candles, notice what the

flame looks like, how it moves and smells. Take a moment to inhale it. If you are putting on special clothes, feel the fabric. How does it feel? Are you putting on perfume or cologne? Take an extra moment to inhale the scent. You get the idea: with anything you are doing, move slightly slower and take a moment to pay attention to what you are seeing, hearing, smelling, feeling, and tasting.

7. KISS MINDFULLY. Rediscover kissing. Tune in to the feeling of your lips and the sensations of your tongues touching (if they do). Notice any judgments, let them be, and come back to being with the feeling of kissing.

59

RELAX, PARENTS,
THE ANSWERS LIE WITHIN

When my wife and I first became parents we were on the hunt for great baby books that would help us be as prepared as we needed to be. I had Benjamin Franklin's voice in my head: "By failing to prepare you are preparing to fail." Some of the books seemed legitimately helpful for nursing, sleeping, getting rid of eye gook, rashes, and how to deal with tantrums. Then we were lucky enough to be invited to a private talk by the famous pediatrician and author Berry Brazelton. Toward the end of his talk he said, "You know, it may just be that the enormous field of childhood parenting books has done parents a disservice. It has sent them the message that they need to look externally to experts to find the answers, when oftentimes the answers lie within; they always have." These were the words I was looking for.

And so it is; parenting is very much about tapping into that space of awareness and tuning into our inner world to nurture the trust that we have what it takes. This isn't a declaration against parenting experts but to temper the all-too-common belief that we can't rely on our intuition to raise our children.

Consider this example. It's bedtime for your child and yet again he is protesting going to sleep. You are exhausted from these recent struggles. As you agree to read one more story, your mind jumps to all the dishes that have piled up and how long it's been since you've been able to spend quality time with your partner. The thoughts arise: "What's wrong with my kid?" "How come Sally in my mothers' group is able to get her kids down on time?" "Maybe it's not my kid, maybe it's me, what's wrong with me?" "I need to find a book on this." As your body tenses up and emotions start bubbling just beneath the surface, the story comes to an end.

If we examine this situation, it's clear that the mind is really thinking, "I'd love to be anywhere *but here* right now," and the fact is, it's working, because the mind is elsewhere. Meanwhile, distress builds.

Let's continue this scenario using your work from *The Now Effect*. As your body tenses up you recognize you're sitting in a space of awareness and choose to tune into the reality of this moment. You ask yourself, "Where am I starting from right now?" As you tap into the triangle of awareness, you find that you're tired, your body is tense, and thoughts of trying to "fix it" are spinning. These facts are not inherently good or bad. As you step out of autopilot, you feel a bit more in control and let out a big breath. You become aware of your child snuggled up against you and thoughts arise of his getting older, making you recognize the preciousness of this moment. As you attune to his experience, you realize that you've been working longer hours lately and haven't seen him as much as usual. The thought arises, "Maybe he just needs a bit more time with me," as you choose to read him one extra story. When the book ends you give him a bit more time by lying down with him and also give yourself permission to rest your eyes.

Stepping into the spaces of awareness while parenting can give you the insights into what really matters and sends the message internally that you can trust yourself.

Remember, you will never be the *perfect parent* so let go of the burden of that fantasy. However, you can be *good enough* as the well-known psychologist Donald Winnicott pointed out. You can apply "See, touch, go" to this too. As soon as you notice yourself drifting, you are present and can shift to tuning back into yourself and your child. Be compassionate with yourself.

now moment

Take a moment to consider how fast kids grow up. More often than not people who have grown kids say, "It all goes by so fast." Consider how you want to be with your kids the next moment you see them. Do you want to be more attentive, more curious, or more loving? Set the intention right now for how you want to be with them. As we know, life becomes routine and it's easy to fall back into old patterns, so practice dipping into these spaces of awareness daily, and in time the Now Effect will take root in your parenting.

60

THE AIKIDO
OF COMMUNICATION

If you propose to speak, always ask yourself, is it true, is it necessary, is it kind? —BUDDHA

Cheryl was thirty-eight years old and a mother of three who worked full-time to find people jobs in the legal industry. In 2010, it wasn't easy; the unemployment rate was at an all-time high, and people were on edge. She went in to work every day and tried to do the best she could. One Monday morning she turned on her computer to find an e-mail from a recent candidate that said, "Dear Cheryl, unless you get me an interview with a company soon, I will have no choice but to call my attorney and sue you and your company as a result of discrimination. I'm sick and tired of being overlooked, and I'm just not going to take it this time." It was a very aggressive e-mail, and she got hooked into a confrontation. She immediately clicked REPLY and wrote an e-mail explaining that she didn't discriminate and in fact hadn't scheduled interviews for anyone. She then told him that she would no longer represent him because of his accusation. She pressed SEND and moved on for the day but couldn't shake the uneasy feeling lingering over her.

The next morning Cheryl realized how reactive her e-mail had been and had the feeling that she needed to hear the man out. In this space of awareness, she knew that he was desperate to get a job. When she reached the office, she called him and said, "I want to understand your thoughts better; tell me what happened from your point of view." She listened to him for thirty minutes, and through this process her heart began to open and her mirror neurons began to fire as she felt his suffering. She said, "After listening to you, I see exactly why this is so painful. It's a brutal job market right now, and if I were in your position I would be frustrated and angry too." The man began to calm down a bit, letting down his defenses, and admitted that he had used the approach with a few other recruiters and that his wife had said that his anger and feeling of victimhood were getting the best of him. Cheryl used the opportunity to redirect the conversation in a more constructive direction: "This interaction didn't work for either of us; I wonder if there's a way to make it better. Are you interested in my professional feedback?" He said yes, and she explained to him that threatening e-mails wouldn't be effective in this job market but that they could work together on brushing up his résumé. As they were about to get off the phone, the man said, "You know, in my entire life I've never been listened to like this before and certainly not by any recruiter. Thank you so much."

When it comes to difficult interactions, it's easy to fall into the default perception that it's you against others, leading you to react in ways that can escalate a difficult situation. When we begin to break free from the delusion of disconnection and appreciate that fundamentally we all want to feel understood and cared about, we can employ a new strategy that can make us black belts at communication.

Morihei Ueshiba was a Japanese martial artist who is best known for founding aikido, a martial art based on peacemaking, kindness, and connection. If someone is coming toward you to attack, you can be passive or avoidant or ignore the attack and make yourself the victim. Or you can fight back and be aggressive or passive-aggressive, making yourself the aggressor. Aikido allows us to see things in a middle way.

We can learn to blend with the energy coming our way, to create a sense of connection and harmony. This approach relates to communication because it begins with dropping into a space of awareness and practicing mindful listening.

Remember, however, that your emotions and mental state can skew your perception and interpretation of another person's intentions. If you walk into a confrontation afraid or angry, it will certainly impact the way you understand what the other person is trying to convey. If you can step back and notice the tension, you are more likely to move into a space of awareness where you can suddenly be more flexible with your responses. This will lead to the option of using the Aikido of Communication.

now moment

Now we're ready to practice the four steps of the Aikido of Communication:

1. ALIGN. That is exactly what Cheryl did. She practiced mind-

ful listening and tried to put herself in her client's shoes. She asked him to speak about his situation because she wanted to understand so she could get a better sense of where he was coming from. When you align with people, you are no longer combating them. Instead, you are aligning with them so that you have a chance to look in the same direction and find common ground.

2. AGREE. This is a practice of empathy in which you put yourself in the other person's shoes to feel what he or she is feeling and continue the process of looking in the same direction. Here is where Cheryl said, "After listening to you, I see exactly why this is so painful. It's a brutal job market right now, and if I were in your position I would be frustrated and angry too." This takes the wind out of the aggression, and now it feels as if you are walking together. You don't have to agree with everything the other person is saying, but responding with empathy helps the interaction.

3. REDIRECT. When two people are walking together side by side and there is no longer any combat, possibilities to redirect the conversation open up. You might say, "It seems that this was a difficult situation for both of us; maybe we can find a solution to make it better." It's as if you took the other person's aggressive energy, stepped alongside it, and used it for good.

4. RESOLVE. Coming to a resolution means finding a solution that is agreeable to both parties or simply agreeing to disagree. Fortunately for Cheryl, the resolution was for her client to accept professional feedback and a chance to improve his résumé. Of course, we can all get stuck in rigid ways of thinking, and conflicts don't always come to a clean and easy ending. At such times we have to recognize when there will be no resolu-

tion and either agree to come back to the issue later or perhaps agree to disagree.

Consider someone with whom you frequently have arguments or frustrating conversations. Our most intimate relationships are often a treasure trove of such experiences. Reflect on a recent argument, and see what happens when you visualize using the Aikido of Communication. How might the situation have been different from the way you handled it? How might you have aligned with the other person? What could you have agreed on? How could you have redirected the conversation? What might have been a resolution?

Try to bring a nonjudgmental curiosity to difficult interactions. Ask yourself, "How would I feel if I were in this person's shoes?" Repeat what the other person says to see if you truly understand, the point he or she is trying to make. If you don't understand, ask the person to say more because you really want to understand. This sends the message that you care, brings defenses down, and paves the way to a better resolution.

61

KEEP YOUR HEART OPEN IN HELL

Be kind, for everyone you meet is fighting a hard battle.

—PLATO

I have always seen stories and metaphors with morals as powerful tools for helping me really get a message on a deeper level. Years ago, when I was beginning my practice as a psychologist, I set up meetings with leading therapists to glean their wisdom so I could start out on the right foot. When I walked into one man's office, we exchanged a few pleasantries, and then I got down to the heart of the matter. I asked him one question: "In your time as a therapist, what has been one of the greatest things you've learned?" He looked up and began to think. After a few moments, he looked back into my eyes and replied, "While people may come in to see me once a week or so, the real therapy happens in their daily lives. I could spend an entire session with a couple trying to explain and enact the therapeutic concept of remaining present, empathic, and compassionate to the other during difficult times, but while this may support them in the moment, the message may or may not stick with them throughout the week. But if I ask, 'Can you keep your heart open in hell?' this is more likely to stay with them and they will be able to grab at it when difficulty arises. Using tools during difficult times is when change really happens."

"Can you keep your heart open in hell?" is a powerful question. It is asking if, when we are entrapped by our unhealthy habits that keep us stuck in perpetual avoidance of what's uncomfortable or foreign, we can drop into a space of awareness and stay with that discomfort, opening up to the presence of another with a sense of compassion and love.

What difference would it make if we were able to put ourselves in another's shoes more often instead of reacting with defensiveness or attacks? What difference would it make if we intentionally sent out informal phrases of kindness to those we were having difficulty with, wishing them well, free from harm, and healthy in body and mind? What difference would it make if we actually allowed ourselves to love or be loved, instead of constantly keeping our feelings at bay in order to feel a false sense of safety?

The question "Can you keep your heart open in hell?" sticks with me during difficult moments in therapy and has also come up in my intimate relationships. It helps me shift away from my automatic behavior of shutting down into one of presence. Learning to keep our hearts open during difficult times in our relationships may just be what is necessary to break free from our negative habitual patterns and transform disconnection into connection.

now moment

Often it's the people who are closest to us that push our buttons the most. Consider right now what it would be like if during one of those difficult moments the phrase "Keep your heart open in hell" ran through your mind. What would be different?

You may choose to make a sign that reads, "Keep your heart open," and put it somewhere where you will see it often.

THE NOW EFFECT LESSONS

John O'Donohue was a priest and poet whose life was cut short in January 2008. Shortly before his death, he was asked if anything haunted him. He replied, "It is the sense of my days running through my fingers like the finest sand and I can't stop it."

Whether our minds like it or not, we all share the common truth that we will not live forever. It is this truth, however, that frees us up to recognize the wonders of everyday life. When we deny the impermanence of our lives, we fall into a routine and don't see the bounty of every day.

Father O'Donohue wished that we would "experience each day as a sacred gift woven around the heart of wonder."

We can't possibly do this if we don't recognize the spaces of awareness all around us that breathe the preciousness of life. It is the very nature of *not* lasting that makes things precious.

As the sand slips through our fingers, we tend to get lost in the details of our lives, losing perspective in the grand scheme of things. In the context of the universe, we are merely a flash in time.

Our moments in this life, in this day, right now, are precious and may even be considered a sacred gift. Occasionally we have "Aha!" moments that give us a window into the wonders that are around us. But because our brains are inclined to make our lives routine, such moments have a tendency to drift into the background or be missed completely. To stay connected to what really matters, we need to cultivate a practice of seeing the choice points all around us to live the life we want.

The second I stepped out of that broken-down limousine in the streets of San Francisco, I was convinced that something had to change in my life. I started going to the gym, engaging in creative activities and turning down invitations to go back to my old patterns. As I picked myself back up, I began to build a community that supported my new aspiration to overcome my conditioning of avoidance and say "Yes!" to life. I sought out people and teachers who were engaged in practices to be more present in their lives. Through this process I continually primed my mind to be more aware of the spaces in my days.

As I continued on this path, I created new memories for my subconscious mind to reference when making snap judgments about what was important and unimportant to me. My worries began to dissipate like clouds, and I was more playful and flexible, experiencing moments of curiosity that connected me to the wonder of this world. I'd notice my mind wandering toward new territory, such as appreciating trees and wondering how they grow. Or noticing a space to close my eyes and listen to the birds chirping, only to reopen my eyes and be in awe of the variety of animals on this planet. I was happy.

As happens in life, the dark clouds came again, and I found myself making a call to an old friend with the hidden hope that I'd fall back into a night of forgetting myself. As I sat at my desk, I listened to the phone ringing, and then he picked up on the other end and said, "Hey, Elisha, long time no talk." My heart quivered as if it were trying to remind me of this space of awareness, this space of choice, this space of opportunity. My thoughts scattered like clouds in the wind, and a new thought arose: "You don't have to be a slave to the past, it's that simple." As my mind found a space of silence, the quiver in my heart continued to remind me that I am worthy of love and in that space I have the choice to treat myself in kind. Gathering my courage, I told my friend I just wanted to check in, hoped he was doing well, and had to go.

We all make our choices in life and can choose a life that is worth living.

Uncovering the wise voice inside you so that it shifts from making rare appearances to becoming the voice from which you see, hear, and speak on a daily basis is the Now Effect. Why not make the choice to open your eyes and your heart to get in touch with what is most important right now?

In this moment, you have the opportunity to make a better life and a better world.

The secret is in the spaces.

DEEPEN YOUR PRACTICE

Deepening your practice with *The Now Effect* is simply about creating space in your day to intentionally engage with a longer practice. The purpose of setting longer periods of time aside for these specific practices is to further prime your mind to drop into those spaces of awareness and clarity more often in your daily life. Studies find that the more intentional attention we give to these practices, the more we see brain change and therefore reprogram a healthier autopilot.

Probably the number one thought that arises in reaction to the notion of creating space for practice is "I don't have time." What would happen if you were aware of this thought, but didn't grasp on to it and then let it fall away? Then ask the question, "Where can I create space for five, ten, fifteen, or more minutes a day to deepen my practice?" See what comes up. Allow "I have no time" to come and go until a new thought arises.

Can you wake up ten minutes early? Is there a space or time at your job where you can stop and practice? Maybe you can even sit in your car after work or before you enter the house? Often, people like to practice later in the evening when the lights are out and there exists a natural stillness.

In this space, you can clear away any possible distractions such as alarms or cell phones. Some people like to have pillows and blankets to make them feel more comfortable when sitting or lying down. Others surround themselves with objects that carry the meaning of calm, wisdom, effectiveness, balance, or even love.

Again, bring a spirit of playfulness and experiment to this. Each part of this section has a link to a five-minute video that you can listen to to get you started. See what works for you. Try one out for a week at a time and if it doesn't feel right, go with another. In time you may feel like increasing your practice to ten, fifteen, or thirty minutes.

Consider in this moment, where you can clear away five minutes a day to start with these practices. If you want to start with more time, go for it.

If time goes by and obstacles arise where you don't practice, know that as soon as you realize this, you are present, in a space of awareness and choice, where you can once again look at your day and see where you can train your mind to be here now.

If you have the time right now, let's give it a go.

THE BODY SCAN

After leading people through the Body Scan, I always ask, "How was that different from how you normally pay attention to your body?" The overwhelming response is "That's assuming that I normally pay attention to it." Living a short distance from our bodies is an epidemic in our culture; yet if our body is a barometer that tells us how we're doing from moment to moment, it would behoove us to develop a greater intimacy with it.

The Body Scan is focused on doing just that.

The following steps will guide you through preparing for the practice and then take you through a step-by-step guide to deepen your connection to the body and train your mind to realize the Now Effect.

preparing for practice

1. Set aside five, ten, twenty, or thirty minutes to sit or lie down and slowly bring awareness to sensations in your body. Move your focus progressively from your feet to your head. Sensations may include heat, coolness, tingling, itchiness, wetness, dryness, pressure, heaviness, lightness, and even pain. If you do this without the video, you can use a timer to remind you when the time is up. Don't worry if you haven't made it through your whole body when the time is up. The purpose isn't to complete the whole body from head to toe, but simply to practice dropping into spaces of awareness and mindfully attending to the direct experience of your body as it is right now.

2. Remember to bring a playful awareness to this practice; when your mind wanders off, think of it as a puppy and practice "See, touch, go." Hold the intention to bring a kind and caring attention, allowing and welcoming whatever is there to be as it is without judgment. You can treat this as a game, starting with a short practice and slowly building up.

3. Be aware of the spaces when you move from one part of your body to the next. Recognize that in this space is a choice to intentionally guide your attention to the next part of your body.

step-by-step instructions

1. MINDFUL CHECK-IN. Notice the position of your body. What emotions are present? What thoughts are filtering through your mind? Are there any judgments or resistance? Is your mind telling you that there are more important things to do? Whatever is there, see if you can just acknowledge it and let it be.

2. THE BREATH AS AN ANCHOR. Begin to gently shift to noticing your body breathing. Imagine that it's the first time you've ever noticed your breath. Where do you feel it? What is the sensation like? Continue this for about a minute or until it feels right to move on.

3. YOUR FEET AND ANKLES. Bring your attention into your feet, and welcome any feelings that are there. As with the rest of this practice, if there are no feelings, notice what it's like to experience no feeling. Before moving up your legs, notice that you are in a space of awareness with the choice to move your attention. Now intentionally move your attention.

4. YOUR LEGS. Slowly guide your awareness up either one leg at a time or both legs at once. Dip your awareness into your body, feeling and allowing what is there. Notice sensations in your calves, shins, knees, and upper legs with the hamstrings and quadriceps. Sense the density of this area of the body. Before

moving on to your hips, again notice the space of awareness between stimulus and response.

5. YOUR HIPS. Become aware of your entire hip region. Notice and open to any sensations in your buttocks, the sides of your hips, and your genitals. If for any reason this area of the body is triggering for you due to past trauma, please be sensitive to that and go at your own pace.

6. YOUR TORSO. You can bring your attention to your back and then move to the front or do the whole area at once. If you choose to do them separately, go up the back vertebra by vertebra and sense any feelings that arise with curiosity and without judgment. When you get to the abdominal region, breathe into your abdomen and notice it expand. Then breathe out and notice it contract. The abdomen and chest are often places where people hold emotions such as fear, love, and restlessness, among others. If you come across any emotions there, see them as simply pieces in the sandbox of your body. Name them and let them be.

7. YOUR SHOULDERS. This is another area that can hold tension. Being with what's here may prime your mind to be more aware of tension you hold in your shoulders during the day, so if you notice that your shoulders are tight, it may trigger your mind into letting them relax. If your mind has been skipping over the space between one part of the body and the next, bring the awareness back now.

8. YOUR FACE AND HEAD. As you scan your face, be aware of any points of pressure. This is often a sign of resisting something. You can let them soften or just notice the sensations as they are.

9. BACK TO THE BREATH. To end the Body Scan, spend another minute riding the breath with your awareness with the same

curiosity and sense of welcoming that you intended throughout the practice.

10. THANK YOURSELF FOR TAKING THIS TIME. This may seem trivial, but it sends the message internally that you care about your well-being and helps sow the seeds of resiliency.

SITTING MEDITATION WITH AWARENESS OF THOUGHTS

The Sitting Meditation with Awareness of Thoughts is an integrative practice that gives you the experience of intentionally bringing your attention to a variety of things, including sounds and thoughts. As we practice relating *to* our thoughts instead of *from* our thoughts, the spaces of awareness begin to open up, producing greater freedom.

www.youtube.com/NowEffect

preparing for practice

1. Set aside five, ten, fifteen, or thirty minutes to sit either in a chair or on the floor. There are six steps to this practice, so depending on the amount of time you allot to this practice, break up each step equally.

2. If you sit on the floor, you can sit on cushions to help your posture. You'll want to have a straight yet comfortable spine to support being awake. If for any reason you are uncomfortable sitting, you can lie down. If you do this without the video, use a timer to remind you when the time is up.

3. Remember to bring some playfulness to this practice, so when your mind wanders off, think of it as a puppy and practice "See, touch, go." Hold the intention to bring a kind and caring attention, allowing and welcoming whatever is there to be as it is without judgment. You can treat this as a game, starting with a short practice and slowly building up.

4. As you breathe, notice the space between one breath and the next and between the moment your mind becomes stimulated to shift to the next part of the practice and actually shifting. Be aware that it is a choice.

5. If you're doing this on your own, that is perfectly fine. The purpose isn't to get through all the steps but simply to play with what's there.

6. If your mind comes up with a story of how there is no time to do a longer practice such as this or you'll get to it at some later time without any specific suggestions as to when, simply see the net effect of that thought. It's the autopilot at work, making it unlikely that you will give yourself the time to do this in the future. Now is the time; it's the only time.

step-by-step instructions

1. MINDFUL CHECK-IN. Begin this practice with a mindful check-in, sensing how you are.

2. THE BREATH AS AN ANCHOR. Use the breath as a means to begin steadying your mind and playing with the wandering mind. Notice the spaces between inhalation and exhalation.

3. FEEL YOUR BODY. Unlike in the Body Scan, in this practice we are noticing the entire field of sensations. There may be some parts

of the body that have more sensation than others; there may be moments when you notice a sensation that increases in intensity, and then, as you get curious and play with it, you watch it gently pass away, demonstrating the impermanent nature of all things.

4. HEAR THE SOUNDS AROUND YOU. Just as we can be aware of the breath and sensations in the body, we can bring awareness to sounds and hearing. Sounds come in the form of pitches, tones, and frequency. A sound also has the quality of coming and going like sensations and the breath. There are also spaces between sounds. As you pay attention to sounds, you may notice images running through your mind that are connected with the sounds. "See, touch, go" with these as you prepare to peer at your thoughts.

5. SEE YOUR THOUGHTS. In the same way that we can be aware of sounds, we can bring attention into the mind to notice our thoughts. This is a bit more abstract, so it helps to use metaphors or images to describe how to do this. Imagine sitting in a dark movie theater and looking at the images and actors talking on the screen. We are not in the movie but watching it. In this same way, watch the appearance and disappearance of thoughts in your mind. As one thought disappears, is there a space before the next one? At times you may notice getting caught up or lost in the story of your thoughts, as we can in a movie too. When this happens, "See, touch, go."

6. THE BREATH AS AN ANCHOR. Come back to where you started, to end this practice.

7. CREATE SOME SIMPLE GESTURE to acknowledge your effort to take this time out. This leaves an imprint in your memory of caring for yourself, which makes it easier to recall.

Loving-kindness practice has been called the healer of fear. Though many know this process as *metta* practice from Buddhist philosophy, the practice of loving-kindness has been found among many peoples, including the Greeks, who called it agape; Jews, who practiced *chesed;* and Christians, who practiced centering prayer. Getting in touch with our hearts is something that millions of people have found helpful when cultivating more kindness toward themselves, their community, and the world.

Note: Notice if any judgments arise: "This can't help me," "I've tried this once in the past or something like it, forget it," or "This sounds woo-woo." Merely be aware of these judgments as strong underlying habits of the mind trying to maintain the status quo. Practice "See, touch, go," and gently bring your attention back to this practice.

In this practice we are cultivating wishes or aspirations, starting with someone you care about. Then we move on to ourselves, then to someone who is neutral, then to someone whom we are having difficulty with, and then to our community and the world. This is not an affirmation practice, we are not telling ourselves something that is not there at the moment; we are simply wishing ourselves and others to be happy, healthy, free from harm, and free from fear. You can come up with your own wishes for yourself, but they should be things you can also wish for others.

You may do this for five, ten, fifteen, or even thirty minutes. If you choose a shorter amount of time, you can begin by doing only the first few steps and building up from there as time goes on.

www.youtube.com/NowEffect

the phrases

The following are some examples of phrases you can use for yourself and others during this practice.

> May I be safe and protected from inner and outer harm.
> May I be truly happy and deeply peaceful.
> May I live my life with ease.
> May I have love and compassion for myself.
> May I love myself completely, just the way I am.
> May I be free.

step-by-step instructions

1. MINDFUL CHECK-IN. Take a seat, feel into your body, and notice how you are doing in this moment, physically and emotionally.
2. A FRIEND. Picture someone who is living that you really care about, someone you are on good terms with and whom it is easy to wish well. You can also choose an animal that you love. With intention, connecting to your heart, repeat the phrases a few times as if you were speaking them to this friend.
3. YOU. Continue by wishing the same phrases for yourself. This may be difficult, as you may feel a lot of pent-up unworthiness. At times a feeling of sadness may arise along with compassion. Take this practice at your own pace, knowing that even experimenting with it is moving you in the direction of greater self-love.

4. AN ACQUAINTANCE. Consider someone you don't know too well, maybe a checkout clerk at the store, a friend of a friend, or a person you seem to see everywhere but have never met. Picture that person in front of you and wish him or her the phrases.

5. A DIFFICULT PERSON. When choosing a difficult person, make sure that he or she is not *the most* difficult person in your life or someone with whom you've experienced extreme trauma. Instead, pick someone you're frustrated or annoyed with. If you're feeling resistance, it may be helpful to reflect upon who actually suffers mentally and physically from resentments and grudges. We can begin to neutralize such feelings with this practice, unlock the door to forgiveness, and begin to heal. See if you can get in touch with your heart in the same way you did for your friend earlier, and wish this person well with the phrases.

6. A COMMUNITY. Some people have a community to which they feel connected. This might be a religious community, a school community, a group of friends, or even your city. Get a sense of the whole community, say, "May we all be well," and then follow with the remaining phrases. You might even consider the connection of all humans on the planet and picture everyone when continuing with the phrases. Imagine: if we all felt well and safe, there likely wouldn't be any need for war. So why not wish it for everyone?

7. MINDFUL CHECK-IN. End this practice with a mindful check-in, thanking yourself for taking the time out of all your daily busyness; this is an act of self-love.

SKY OF AWARENESS MEDITATION

The intention of the Sky of Awareness Meditation is to cultivate a larger open-mindedness and give you the experience of how your awareness truly is. You'll be opening your attention to an unfolding of sounds, thoughts, body, and breath. The wonderful thing about this practice is that you can do it anywhere and anytime because the environment is the only equipment needed for practice.

www.youtube.com/NowEffect

preparing for practice

1. Set aside five, ten, fifteen, or thirty minutes to sit, stand, or lie down. There are six steps to this practice, so depending on the amount of time you allot to it, allot the same amount of time to each step.

2. Remember to bring a sense of curiosity and playfulness to this practice, treating it as an experiment that includes neither good nor bad. Hold the intention to bring a kind and caring attention, allowing and welcoming whatever is there to be as it is without judgment. You can treat this as a game, devoting a short time to it and then slowly building up.

3. If you're doing this without audio guidance, that is perfectly fine. As always, the purpose isn't to get through the entire practice but to play with your attention, continuing to gently bring it back to the present moment.

4. If your mind sends this to the bottom of your to-do list, in-

vestigate whether that is really what you want to do or if that is your autopilot.

step-by-step instructions

1. MINDFUL CHECK-IN. As with previous practices, start by acknowledging what's present in this space physically, emotionally, and mentally.

2. SOUNDS. Whereas with other practices we began with the breath, this is going to be different. Take a moment to imagine that your awareness is as big as the physical space you are in right now. Notice the sounds rising and passing away. Then allow your awareness to go beyond the borders of the room, spreading throughout the sky. It is infinitely expansive, without boundaries.

3. THOUGHTS. Within this vast and wide awareness there are also thoughts. Proceed by opening and welcoming the thoughts that are there along with the sounds. Just practice allowing what's there to be as it is.

4. BODY. Consider for a moment that your body is simply a collection of physical sensations that come and go within this sky of awareness. Allow the image of a physical body with boundaries to dissolve and the feelings that are there to filter within this awareness along with thoughts and sounds. There is plenty of room for all of it, and you are just watching, experiencing, and opening the space.

5. BREATH. Now bring in the breath and practice open-mindedness,

DEEPEN YOUR PRACTICE   239

allowing all of the phenomena to shift and change, appear and disappear within your sky of awareness.

6. MAKE A SMALL GESTURE INWARD, thanking yourself for taking this time out for practice.

SEEING THE PERSON

Seeing the Person is a five-to-ten-minute practice that I've adapted from Joanna Macy's work in *World as Lover, World as Self.* I was originally guided through this by Jack Kornfield, and my experience was powerful enough for me to bring it into my work with other people. I've used it in groups, with couples, and with a number of other people to help them truly see another person. It's meant to cultivate a sense of intimacy between two people and dissolve the delusion of disconnection. If you currently have an intimate partner whom you feel safe with, I suggest trying this with him or her. If not, you can pick a friend. If you'd rather do this alone, you can also just play with this and slowly build up to doing it with another person. There's a difference between reading about how to see a person and actually doing it.

www.youtube.com/NowEffect

step-by-step instructions

1. Find a partner whose eyes you can look into for the next five or ten minutes. If you don't have a partner or don't feel comfortable doing this with another person, close your eyes and picture someone you care about.

2. Sit facing each other, and take a few deep breaths in this shared space. It's rare that we intimately look into another person's eyes, so discomfort, embarrassment, or laughter is completely natural. You can practice "See, touch, go" with this as it occurs.

3. LOVING-KINDNESS. As you look into the other person's eyes, become aware of his or her beauty. Open your mind to the person's strengths. Behind his or her eyes are invaluable qualities of intelligence, love, compassion, determination, and wisdom. The person may not even be aware of the power he or she holds. As you look into the person's eyes, begin to wish him or her well, to be happy, safe, and protected from inner and outer harm and free from the fear that binds him or her. As you do this practice, know that what you may be feeling is the heart of loving-kindness.

4. Close your eyes, breathe a few times, then reopen your eyes.

5. COMPASSION. Look into the other person's eyes once again and see the history behind the person, the gradual accumulation of suffering, the depth of sorrow and pain that lies within. The person has certainly lived with his or her own perceived failures, losses, unworthiness, disappointments, and loneliness. You cannot fix his or her pain, but see if you can connect with your heart, opening to and being with what's there. Imagine the person as your own child, frightened and alone; how would you hold the child in your mind's eye? As you do this practice, know that what you may be feeling is the heart of compassion, which is essential to heal any relationship.

6. Close your eyes, breathe a few times, then reopen your eyes.

7. JOY. Look into the other person's eyes once again and see all

of his or her happy moments, triumphs, and experiences of adventure as a child, the joy and creativity that live within, and the times of authentic laughter filled with freedom. Now imagine how you both have these joys and how you might partner to overcome obstacles, pick each other up during moments of difficulty, and bring joy and happiness into the life you will have together. See the potential for happiness in the person and know that you may now be experiencing a connection of feeling a selfless joy for another person's joy.

8. Close your eyes, breathe a few times, then reopen your eyes.

9. WISDOM. Look into the other person's eyes one last time and see the awareness that lies behind the eyes from which they're viewing you. Know that your minds are connected in the big mind of awareness that we all share. Even though all things in life seem to come and go, this collective consciousness remains the same. Sit and feel into it; this is the seat of your wise self.

10. When you are done, take another few breaths and acknowledge your partner in whatever ways feel natural to you.

FIVE-STEP CHEAT SHEET

1. **WHEREVER YOU ARE, THAT IS THE ENTRY POINT.** Practice moving out of autopilot and seeing the spaces of awareness wherever you are throughout the day. We can begin to notice the spaces where we get hooked, see the moment as a choice point, and consider a wiser perspective. As you practice and repeat, uncovering the wise voice inside, it will shift from the voice you hear only during rare moments to the voice from which you consistently see, hear, and speak to cultivate a more enduring Now Effect.

2. **PRIME YOUR MIND.** The more you practice, the more your mind is inclined to notice the spaces. Sometimes it's helpful to have signposts to help bring us back to the present moment and reinforce a way of being to which we aspire. Just as signs on the road can help remind us to slow down or be aware of children crossing, we can make and post reminders that say, "Breathe," "Where am I starting from right now?" "Say 'Yes!'" "STOP," "Play," "Welcome," "Just like me," "Keep your heart open," or "What is most important right now?" By doing so, you prime

your mind and heart to live what's next with more playfulness, acceptance, kindness, nonjudgment, openness, and compassion.

3. CHANGE YOUR MIND. Be on the lookout for the unhealthy mind traps and automatic negative thoughts that don't serve you. Understand that thoughts are not facts and you can choose to orient your mind toward the good.

4. SEE, TOUCH, GO. As you integrate the practices into your life, expect to stray; this is a natural tendency of the mind. When this happens, practice "See, touch, go" over and over again. See where you went, touch it, and gently guide yourself back to your life.

5. GET CONNECTED. The truth is, we are not islands, and we function better and have greater opportunities for success when we're part of a community. Find a friend, a colleague, or a family member, or connect with the greater Now Effect community to stay connected, thrive, and sustain your playful discipline to this life practice.

Appendix C

———

TRAINING GROUND CHEAT SHEET

Take this list with you wherever you go, and pull it out to look at when you have a free moment. Pick one of the practices on the list, and make it a Now Moment. Sprinkling these five short practices into the spaces of your day can change the rest of your life.

1. THE BREATH AS AN ANCHOR. Bring awareness to the breath to bring you into the now. Play with your wandering mind, gently and nonjudgmentally guiding it back each time.

2. MINDFUL CHECK-IN. Ask, "Where am I starting from right now?" Check in with your thoughts, sensations, and emotions; practice welcoming whatever is there, whether it's comfortable, uncomfortable, or neutral.

3. STOP. **S**top, **T**ake a breath, **O**bserve your experience, **P**roceed with what's most important.

4. GO. Bring mindfulness to any movement; for just a few minutes, practice a few gentle opening yoga poses.

5. ACE. During difficult moments, practice bringing **A**wareness to your thoughts, sensations, and emotions, then **C**ollecting attention on the breath, and finally **E**xpanding and grounding awareness throughout your entire body. Then bring an open curiosity to whatever discomfort is there.

Acknowledgments

Many people have helped shape the teachings and experiences that have led to *The Now Effect*. Perhaps my greatest teacher and source of support is my wife, Stefanie Goldstein, who constantly challenges me to find that space between stimulus and response where I have a choice to become aware of my own innate wisdom and love. I also want to thank her for very graciously and patiently allowing me to disappear at times while I was working on *The Now Effect*. Everyone should be so lucky as to have a partner like her. My sons, Lev and Bodhi, continue to help me tap into my beginner's mind, priming me to be present and illuminating the wonders of everyday life. I want to express my gratitude to my parents, Jan, Jane, Steve, and Bonnie, for the years of support and guidance and their unwavering belief in me. My sisters, Yaffa, Batsheva, and Shira, and brother, Ari, have also been a tremendous source of inspiration and love. I'm grateful to Marion and Matt Solomon for their guidance and support both personally and professionally, to my in-laws Judy and George Nassif, for their encouragement and support, and also to my in-laws Audrey and Karl Jacobs and Randy and Marie Kessel.

I wouldn't have been on this path of mindfulness without my

teachers, friends, and colleagues, who through their direct guidance have helped me live a more mindful life both personally and professionally: Bob Stahl, Trudy Goodman, Mark Feenstra, Daniel Siegel, Jon Kabat-Zinn, Jack Kornfield, Susan Kaiser Greenland, Tara Brach, Sylvia Boorstein, Sharon Salzberg, Roger Nolan, Christiane Wolf, Steve Hickman, Pat Ogden, Kelley McCabe, Jim Gimian, Barry Boyce, Lienhard Valentin, Genie Palmer, Kate Wolf-Pizor, Kathleen Wall, Lidia Zylowska, Alan Marlatt, and Zindel Segal. Thank you to Chade-Meng Tan, Tim Ryan, Richard Shankman, and Kyra Bobinet for allowing me to interview them and for thier great efforts in bringing mindfulness to business, politics, education, and health care.

It has also been a profound privilege to work with my patients and students, who have trusted me enough to let me into some of the deepest areas of their lives, have given me permission to use some of their stories in this book (with pseudonyms), and have been some of my greatest teachers.

Thank you to John Grohol, the CEO of PsychCentral.com; Mark Dombeck of MentalHelp.net; Alana Kornfeld at The Huffington Post; and Barry Boyce of Mindful.org for graciously inviting me to write for them on mindfulness and psychotherapy. I am also grateful to the regular readers of my blogs along with those who drop in from time to time. Your comments, questions, and stories have greatly influenced my life.

A long list of friends, family, colleagues, and students have read the manuscript, added input at various stages, and given me invaluable feedback: Ari Klaristenfeld, Beatrice Dumin, Susan Kaiser Greenland, Mark Feenstra, Daniel Siegel, Stefanie Goldstein, Christine Brooks, Bonnie Goldstein, Jan Goldstein, Steve Nelson, Therese Borchard, Jeffrey Schwartz, Rebecca Gladding, and Stephanie Tade.

Special thanks to Sheila Oakes, who provided additional editorial support, and to Paul Martini for his wonderful artwork.

Deep bows to my fantastic literary agent and friend, Stephanie Tade, who has shared the passion and dedication to bring transformative material into this world. I feel truly blessed to have our connection. When we set out on this project, we were looking for the publisher that would be the best support for its vision. Finding Johanna Castillo at Atria Books, along with Amy Tannenbaum, has helped transform this book from good to great. I cannot thank Stephanie, Johanna, and Amy enough for helping give life to *The Now Effect*.

Notes

CHAPTER 1: THE WISDOM IN GOLF BALLS

The story of the professor and the golf balls is one that has made its way around the Internet. After an extensive and exhaustive search, it doesn't appear to have any acknowledged source.

CHAPTER 2: PAYING ATTENTION TO YOUR INTENTION

In his book *The Developing Mind* (New York: Guilford Press, 1999), Daniel Siegel, MD, lays out his theory about how all the disorders in the *Diagnostic and Statistical Manual of Mental Disorders* (*DSM*) can be seen through the lens of chaos, rigidity, or both. He is the pioneer of interpersonal neurobiology and has had a significant impact on my work. You can find more about Dan at www.drdansiegel.com.

The idea of attention and intention being the two pillars of change is an old concept that has been seen in many of the world's wisdom traditions. More recently, Shauna Shapiro and Gary Schwartz laid it out in their model for health change in "Intentional Systemic Mindfulness: An Integrative Model for Self-Regulation and Health," *Advances in Mind-Body Medicine* 16, no. 2 (Spring 2000): 128–134. See also Tara Brach, *Radical Acceptance* (New York: Bantam, 2003), and Daniel Siegel, *The Mindful Brain* (New York: Norton, 2007).

CHAPTER 5: SEE, TOUCH, GO

Matthew A. Killingsworth and Daniel T. Gilbert conducted the study "A Wandering Mind Is an Unhappy Mind," *Science* 330, no. 6006 (2010): 932. You can find out more about this experiment at www.trackyourhappiness.org.

CHAPTER 7: SAY "YES!"

Jack Kent wrote the wonderful book *There's No Such Thing as a Dragon* (New York: Dragonfly Books, 2009). I am indebted to this wonderful story, as it has touched many people I've worked with.

After Tara Brach published her book *Radical Acceptance* (New York: Bantam, 2004), there was at times confusion about the word "acceptance." Some people thought it meant you have to be okay with what's there. Acceptance simply implies that you acknowledge the reality of what's in this present moment, whether it's pleasant, unpleasant, or neutral. I am deeply indebted to her work in mindfulness and psychotherapy. You can find more about her work at www.tarabrach.com.

CHAPTER 8: WHERE AM I STARTING FROM?

The "mindful check-in" was first coined by my friend, colleague, and mentor Bob Stahl, PhD. It was included in Bob Stahl and Elisha Goldstein, *A Mindfulness-Based Stress Reduction Workbook* (Oakland, Calif.: New Harbinger, 2010). You can find more about Bob at www.mind fulnessprograms.com.

CHAPTER 9: FEEL THE SPACES IN YOUR BODY

My friend and colleague Pat Ogden is the founder of sensorimotor psychotherapy and a pioneer in the field of psychosomatic approaches to trauma and well-being. See more at www.sensorimotorpsycho therapy.org.

CHAPTER 10: IF YOU CAN NAME IT, YOU CAN TAME IT

"If you can name it, you can tame it" is an adaptation of "Name it to tame it," which was first seen in *The Developing Mind* then in *Mindsight* and *The Whole-Brain Child*, by my friend and colleague Dan Siegel, MD.

In 2007 Matthew D. Lieberman, Naomi I. Eisenberger, Molly J. Crockett, Sabrina M. Tom, Jennifer H. Pfeifer, and Baldwin M. Way published the study "Putting Feelings into Words: Affect Labeling Disrupts Amygdala Activity in Response to Affective Stimuli," *Psychological Science* 18, no. 5 (2007): 421–428. They showed two sets of pictures to people, each showing an angry face and a fearful face. Underneath one set of photos were the names "Dick" and "Jane," and underneath the other were the words "anger" and "fear." They found that the people who saw the pictures of the faces connected with the emotion words showed an increase in activity in the prefrontal region and a decrease in activity in the amygdala, or "fear circuit." This is basically the neuroscience of "If you can name it, you can tame it."

CHAPTER 15: IT'S LIKE THIS . . . AND THIS TOO

Ajahn Chah was a Thai meditation master who used to say, *"Ben yung nee"* ("It's like this"). I have had many students, teachers, friends, and colleagues who have benefited from bringing this simple phrase into their life.

Many people use the word "mind" under the assumption that there is a general understanding of its definition. However, there are various understandings of "mind," some not differentiating from the definition of "brain." In my experience, Daniel Siegel, MD (*The Developing Mind*), and Jeffrey Schwartz, MD, and Rebecca Gladding, MD (*You Are Not Your Brain*), provide the clearest definitions of "mind" and "brain." Daniel Siegel gathered a group of research scientists from many different disciplines, all of whom agreed that "a core aspect of the mind can be defined as an embodied and relational process that regulates the flow of energy and information." To further clarify, in their recent book *You Are Not Your Brain* (New York: Avery, 2011), Jeffrey Schwartz, MD, and Rebecca Gladding, MD, say that the brain receives inputs and generates the *passive* side of experience, whereas the mind is *active*, focusing attention and making decisions. They wrote, "The brain puts out the call, the mind decides whether to listen . . . [with awareness] you have a choice in whether or not to respond when your brain puts out the call."

CHAPTER 19: MEMORY MATTERS

Find more about how much people are looking at their various digital screens in the Nielsen Company, *A2/M2 Three Screen Report, 1st Quarter 2009,* http://blog.nielsen.com/nielsenwire/wp-content/uploads/2009/05/nielsen_threescreenreport_q109.pdf.

CHAPTER 21: TOP TEN HIT LIST

Zindel Segal, Mark Williams, and John Teasdale created Mindfulness-Based Cognitive Therapy and published their first book on it, *Mindfulness-Based Cognitive Therapy for Depression: A New Approach to Preventing Relapse* (New York: Guilford Press), in 2002. To find out more about the evidence-based research behind this eight-week course, go to www.mbct.com/Research_Main.htm.

For more on the automatic thoughts questionnaire, see Steven D. Hollon and Philip C. Kendall, "Cognitive Self-Statements in Depression: Development of an Automatic Thoughts Questionnaire," *Cognitive Therapy and Research* 4, no. 4 (1980): 383–395.

CHAPTER 22: YOUR MIND TRAPS

Portia Nelson's poem "There's a Hole in My Sidewalk" (Hillsboro, Oreg.: Beyond Words, 1993) epitomizes the process of not only how we get out of our mind traps but change itself.

CHAPTER 26: NOW AT WORK

In 2006 the American Psychological Association came out with "Multitasking: Switching Costs," which turned our current perception of multitasking as a path of efficiency and effectiveness on its head. For more information, see www.apa.org/research/action/multi task.aspx.

PART IV: PRIMING YOUR MIND FOR GOOD

Tiffany A. Ito, Jeff T. Larsen, N. Kyle Smith, and John T. Cacioppo conducted the study "Negative Information Weighs More Heavily on the Brain: The Negativity Bias in Evaluative Categorizations," *Journal of Personality and Social Psychology* 75, no. 4 (1998): 887–900, in which they showed thirty-three participants pictures meant to arouse positive feelings, neutral feelings, and negative feelings. Though the positive and negative feelings both activated greater activity in the brain, the negative events aroused the most of all.

John Gottman has written extensively on marriage and relationships. You can learn more about his work at www.gottman.com. Gottman and Robert Levenson published their first study in 1992, "Marital Processes Predictive of Later Dissolution: Behavior, Physiology, and Health," *Journal of Personality and Social Psychology* 63, no. 2: 221–233. Ten years later, in 2002, they published their second study, "A Two-Factor Model for Predicting When a Couple Will Divorce: Exploratory Analyses Using 14-Year Longitudinal Data," *Family Process* 41, no. 1: 83–96, and found 94 percent accuracy on who would stay together and who would be separated based on the earlier scoring of those couples for fifteen minutes.

CHAPTER 28: BE KIND WHENEVER POSSIBLE. IT IS ALWAYS POSSIBLE.

Daniel Ladinsky is the truly remarkable translator of the deeply profound writings of the fourteenth-century Persian poet Hafiz. "It Felt Love" can be found in *The Gift* (New York: Penguin, 1999).

CHAPTER 30: I THINK I CAN, I THINK I CAN

Watty Piper's classic story, which most of us read growing up, *The Little Engine That Could* (New York: Platt & Munk, 1976), inspires us to move forward in the face of adversity to recognize the opportunity that's there.

The late Rick Snyder was one of the first to pave a scholarly path investigating hope in "Hypothesis: There Is Hope," in *Handbook of Hope Theory, Measures, and Applications,* ed. C. R. Snyder (San Diego: Academic Press, 2002), pp. 3–21.

CHAPTER 32: COUNT YOUR BLESSINGS

Robert A. Emmons and Michael E. McCullough are psychologists who conducted a research study, "Counting Blessings Versus Burdens: An Experimental Investigation of Gratitude and Subjective Well-Being in Daily Life," *Journal of Personality and Social Psychology* 84, no. 2 (2003): 377–389, that found that over the course of ten weeks, those who counted their blessings scored higher on well-being scales than those who counted burdens or neutral events.

CHAPTER 36: THE SEEDS OF RESILIENCY

I'm deeply indebted to the work of Jon Kabat-Zinn for being a pioneer in bringing mindfulness to the West in a palatable form. I'm also indebted to Richard Davidson's incredible research into the neurobiological correlates of mindfulness, which has been the groundwork for its acceptance in many of our institutions. Richard J. Davidson, Jon Kabat-Zinn, Jessica Schumacher, Melissa Rosenkranz, Daniel Muller, Saki F. Santorelli, Ferris Urbanowski, Anne Harrington, Katherine Bonus, and John F. Sheridan worked together to produce the groundbreaking study "Alterations in Brain and Immune Function Produced by Mindfulness Meditation," *Psychosomatic Medicine* 65, no. 4 (2003): 564–570. Since this time there has been an exponential increase in the amount of research in the field of mindfulness and neuroscience.

CHAPTER 37: HI, I'M YOUR BRAIN

The term "integrated brain" is at the foundation of interpersonal neurobiology (IPNB). See more at www.drdansiegel.com/about/interpersonal_neurobiology.

In 2005, Sara W. Lazar, PhD, an instructor at Harvard Medical School, published research along with Catherine E. Kerr, Rachel H. Wasserman, Jeremy R. Gray, Douglas N. Greve, Michael T. Treadway, Metta McGarvey, Brian T. Quinn, Jeffery A. Dusek, Herbert

Benson, Scott L. Rauch, Christopher I. Moore, and Bruce Fischl, "Meditation Experience Is Associated with Increased Cortical Thickness," *NeuroReport* 16, no. 17: 1893–1897. They found a measurable difference in the brains of people who practiced meditation compared to those who didn't. Using MRI brain scans, she found thicker regions in the frontal cortex in the meditation group. Additionally, she found a thicker insula, which is involved in sensing internal sensations and is thought to be a critical structure in the perception of emotional feelings.

CHAPTER 40: THE NARRATOR

In 2007 Norman A. S. Farb, Zindel V. Segal, Helen Mayberg, Jim Bean, Deborah McKeon, Zainab Fatima, and Adam K. Anderson published the study "Attending to the Present: Mindfulness Meditation Reveals Distinct Neural Modes of Self-Reference," *Social Cognitive and Affective Neuroscience* 2, no. 4: 313–322. This study showed us where the story of *me* resides in our brains.

In 2010 Farb and his colleagues conducted a follow-up study, "Minding One's Emotions: Mindfulness Training Alters the Neural Expression of Sadness," *Emotion* 10, no. 1: 25–33, showing that activating the experiential area of the brain is what regular mindfulness practitioners do when exposed to sad scenes, rather than engaging with the narrative area, which can lead to rumination and inevitably depression.

CHAPTER 41: FREE YOUR MIND

In 2001 Andreas K. Engel, Pascal Fries, and Wolf Singer published "Dynamic Predictions: Oscillations and Synchrony in Top-Down Processing," *Nature Reviews Neuroscience* 2, no. 10: 704–716, using the word "enslave" to describe how top-down processing can control our perception.

CHAPTER 43: YOUR INTUITIVE BRAIN

The gambling experiment is found in Antoine Bechara, Hanna Damasio, Daniel Tranel, and Antonio R. Damasio, "Deciding Advantageously Before Knowing the Advantageous Strategy," *Science* 274, no. 5304 (February 1997): 1293–1295. See more in Antonio Damasio, *Descartes' Error: Emotion, Reason, and the Human Brain* (New York: HarperCollins, 1994).

CHAPTER 44: WIRED FOR EMPATHY AND COMPASSION

The old saying "Monkey see, monkey do" now has neuroscience behind it. In 1996 Vittorio Gallese, Luciano Fadiga, Leonardo Fogassi, and Giacomo Rizzolatti published "Action Recognition in the Premotor Cortex," *Brain* 119, no. 2: 593–609. This work has been built on by Marco Iacoboni at UCLA (see http://iacoboni.bmap.ucla.edu) and V. S. Ramachandran at UCSD (see http://cbc.ucsd.edu/ramabio.html).

In *The Mindful Brain: Reflection and Attunement in the Cultivation of Well-Being* (New York: Norton, 2007), Daniel Siegel laid out a proposal making the case that harnessing the social circuitry of our brains enables us to develop an attuned relationship with ourselves.

PART VI: WORKING WITH DIFFICULT EMOTIONS

Coleman Barks is the most widely read translator of the thirteenth-century Sufi poet Rumi. He translated one of the most widely spread Rumi books, *The Essential Rumi: Jalal al-Din Rumi* (San Francisco: HarperSanFrancisco, 1995), among many others.

Franz Kafka was an influential German novelist who wrote, among other things, *The Great Wall of China and Other Pieces* (London: Secker and Warburg, 1946).

CHAPTER 52: ANGER: CONSTRUCTIVE, DESTRUCTIVE, OR BOTH?

In 1995 Daniel Goleman first published his influential book *Emotional Intelligence* (New York: Bantam), challenging people to understand the importance of attuning to their emotions in everyday life. Since then there has been an exponential rise in exploring emotional intelligence in psychology, business, sports, and politics, among other disciplines. In 2003 Goleman published *Destructive Emotions: A Scientific Dialogue with the Dalai Lama* (New York: Bantam), helping us understand new ways of relating to our difficult emotions.

PART VII: GETTING CONNECTED

In 2006 I published a study called "Sacred Moments: Implications on Well-Being and Stress," *Journal of Clinical Psychology* 63, no. 10: 1001–1019. In addition to showing statistically significant positive changes in well-being and stress reduction from simply doing a mindfulness-based practice for five minutes a day, five days a week for three weeks, one of the more interesting findings was in qualitative interviews. The people who made the most significant changes all separately reported that the best word to describe their experience was "connection." That led me to believe that cultivating a sense of connection may be at the source of well-being.

CHAPTER 53: THE BIGGEST DISEASE

Father Gregory Boyle has done amazing work in developing programs for the lower socioeconomic community and creating job programs for gang members. In 2010 he published a wonderful book, *Tattoos on the Heart* (New York: Simon & Schuster).

CHAPTER 54: DISCONNECTION IS DELUSION

David Bohm was an American-born quantum physicist who made contributions in several fields. In 1951 he published *Quantum Theory* (New York: Prentice Hall), which helped us understand the physical basis of the interconnection of all things.

CHAPTER 55: THE SCIENCE OF CONNECTION

Nicholas Christakis and Jason Fowler conducted a meta-analysis in their study "The Spread of Obesity in a Large Social Network over 32 Years," *The New England Journal of Medicine* 357 (July 26, 2007): 370–379. Though their finding of emotional contagion has its critics, the idea supporting our social interconnection continues to fascinate people. They joined John Cacioppo to explore how loneliness can spread in the study "Alone in the Crowd: The Structure and Spread of Loneliness in a Large Social Network," *Journal of Personality and Social Psychology* 97, no. 6 (2009): 977–991.

CHAPTER 56: WHY ARE YOU WAITING?

Joanna Macy describes her wonderful practice of interpersonal connection in *World as Lover, World as Self* (New York: Parallax Press, 2005).

APPENDIX A: DEEPEN YOUR PRACTICE

THE BODY SCAN

Jon Kabat-Zinn, the founder of Mindfulness-Based Stress Reduction (MBSR), created the program to start with a Body Scan practice. I will be forever indebted to him for his influential work in this field.

Sharon Salzberg is a pioneer who has played a crucial role in bringing the practice of loving-kindness to the West. You can learn more about her at www.sharonsalzberg.com.

SKY OF AWARENESS MEDITATION

Though *The Now Effect* is a secular book, it draws from many wisdom traditions. A reference to making your mind as vast as a sky can be found in the Buddhist scripture *Majjhima Nikaya*, in which the Buddha says, "Develop a mind that is vast like space, where experiences both pleasant and unpleasant can appear and disappear without conflict, struggle, or harm. Rest in a mind like vast sky."

Bibliography

Brach, T. *Radical Acceptance*. New York: Bantam, 2004.

Chödrön, P. *Taking the Leap*. Boston: Shambhala Publications, 2010.

Emerson, R. W. *Ralph Waldo Emerson: Collected Poems and Translations*. New York: Penguin, 1994.

Frankl, V. *Man's Search for Meaning*. Boston: Beacon Press, 2000.

Hafiz. *The Gift,* trans. D. Ladinsky. New York: Penguin, 1999.

Heschel, A. J. *God in Search of Man: A Philosophy of Judaism*. New York: Farrar, Straus and Giroux, 1955.

Kabat-Zinn, J. *Full Catastrophe Living: Using the Wisdom of Your Body and Mind to Face Stress, Pain, and Illness*. New York: Delta, 1990.

Kabir. *Kabir: Ecstatic Poems,* trans. R. Bly. Boston: Beacon, 2004.

Kaiser-Greenland, S. *The Mindful Child*. New York: Free Press, 2010.

Kent, J. *There's No Such Thing as a Dragon*. New Mexico: Dragonfly Books, 1993.

Kornfield, J. *After the Ecstasy, the Laundry*. New York: Bantam, 2000.

———. *A Path with Heart*. New York: Bantam, 1993.

———. *The Wise Heart*. New York: Bantam, 2008.

Lao-tzu. *The Way of Life,* trans. W. Bynner. New York: Penguin, 1944.

Nhat Hanh, T. *Anger: Wisdom for Cooling the Flames*. New York: Berkley, 2001.

————. *Creating True Peace: Ending Violence in Yourself, Your Family, Your Community, and the World*. New York: Simon & Schuster, 2001.

Oliver, M. *New and Selected Poems*. Boston: Beacon Books, 1992.

Pattakos, A. *Prisoners of Our Thoughts: Viktor Frankl's Principles for Discovering Meaning in Life and Work*. San Francisco: Berrett-Koehler, 2008.

Rumi. *The Soul of Rumi*, trans. C. Barks. San Francisco: Harper San-Francisco, 2001

Salzberg, S. *A Heart as Wide as the World*. Boston: Shambhala, 1997.

————. *Lovingkindness*. Boston: Shambhala, 2002.

Segal, Z. V., J. M. G. Williams, J. D. Teasdale, and J. Kabat-Zinn. *The Mindful Way Through Depression*. New York: Guilford Press, 2007.

Shapiro, S., and L. Carlson. *The Art and Science of Mindfulness: Integrating Mindfulness into Psychology and the Helping Professions*. Washington, DC: APA Books, 2009.

Siegel, D. J. *The Mindful Brain*. New York: W. W. Norton, 2007.

————. *Mindsight: The New Science of Personal Transformation*. New York: Bantam, 2009.

Stahl, R., and E. Goldstein. *A Mindfulness-Based Stress Reduction Workbook*. Oakland, Calif.: New Harbinger, 2010.

Thoreau, H. *Walden*. New York: Simon and Brown, 2011

Tolle, E. *The Power of Now*. New York: New World Library, 1999.

Walcott, D. *Collected Poems*. New York: Farrar, Straus and Giroux, 1987.

Additional Resources

For more information or to purchase the following CDs and MP3 albums, visit www.elishagoldstein.com or www.drsgoldstein.com. You can also purchase them at www.amazon.com.

Mindful Solutions for Stress, Anxiety, and Depression
Mindful Solutions for Addiction and Relapse Prevention
Mindful Solutions for Success and Stress Reduction at Work

Mindfulness Web Sites

Elisha Goldstein: www.elishagoldstein.com
A Mindfulness-Based Stress Reduction Workbook: mbsrwork book.com
Center for Mindfulness at University of Massachusetts Medical School: www.umassmed.edu/cfm
Mind & Life Institute: www.mindandlife.org

Mindful Awareness Research Center (MARC): http://marc
.ucla.edu

Mindsight Institute: www.mindsightinstitute.com

Bob Stahl: www.mindfulnessprograms.com

The Inner Kids Foundation: www.innerkids.org

InsightLA: www.insightla.org

eMindful: www.emindful.com

Mindfulness-Based Programs

Mindfulness-Based Stress Reduction (MBSR) programs abound throughout the United States as well as internationally. If you're interested in joining a program near you, check out the regional and international directory at the Center for Mindfulness at the University of Massachusetts Medical School's Web site: www.umassmed
.edu/cfm/mbsr.

Mindfulness-Based Cognitive Therapy (MBCT) programs to prevent depressive relapse are available in many major cities of the United States. There is no current directory, so type it into your favorite search engine along with your city and see what comes up.

Mindfulness Meditation Centers
and Weekly Sitting Groups

To find mindfulness meditation centers and weekly sitting groups in the United States, consult the following Web sites, which also offer lists of international meditation centers:

For the West Coast, Spirit Rock Meditation Center, www
.spiritrock.org

For the East Coast, Insight Meditation Society, www
.dharma.org

If you haven't already done so, take this moment to connect to *The Now Effect* community at www.elishagoldstein.com. This will provide you with the fundamental support to incorporate *The Now Effect* into your life.

- Get daily Now Moment reminders that prime your mind toward the principles in this book.

- Engage in a weekly newsletter that connects you to essential information, practices, and events.

- Get access to a free live monthly call with Elisha Goldstein, PhD, to go deeper and to get your important questions answered.